ABOUT
THE AUTHORS

FAIRFAX DOWNEY

Fairfax Downey is the author of three adult books on the Scribner list, and numerous magazine articles and stories.

He is also the author of a number of books for teen-age boys and girls, many of which have been illustrated by Paul Brown.

Mr. Downey lives in New York City. His interest in horses began when he owned a horse as a boy, and went on through his service in the Field Artillery.

PAUL BROWN

Paul Brown is one of the leading sporting artists of the country. He has a number of adult books on the Scribner list, as well as books for young people of all ages.

This book has been a true collaboration between author and artist, as they have worked together on it from the beginning.

HORSES OF DESTINY

BY

FAIRFAX DOWNEY
AND
PAUL BROWN

With pen-and-ink illustrations by
PAUL BROWN

1949 - NEW YORK
CHARLES SCRIBNER'S SONS

TO

SQUADRON "A"

NEW YORK

CONTENTS

What form of life lower than our own has served humanity as the horse has served it? He has played bravely his part on a thousand fields of battle, facing war's appalling horror, and moved to his task by no hope of glory. He has helped build the world's great cities, their temples, their palaces, their libraries, their universities. He has toiled on the railways of the nations. He has been a partner in the rearing of our homes. He has been the swift messenger of joy and sorrow. He has carried us through many happy hours of recreation. He has stood ready to die in our service when we asked it.

Francis H. Rowley: THE HORSES OF HOMER

BUCEPHALUS

CHARGER OF ALEXANDER THE GREAT

THE black yearling from Thessaly snorted and reared, dragging handlers who clung to his bridle off their feet. Their utmost efforts could not control the powerful horse, and cavalry inspectors reluctantly waved him away, rejected.

A boy, barely sixteen, shouted fiercely in protest, "I can ride him!"

Philip, the lame king of Macedon, stared at his son, Alexander. "If you can't, will you pay his price of thirteen talents?" Philip demanded. The boy nodded, and his father promised, "By the same token, if you can ride him, he's yours."

Alexander took the bridle and turned the horse to face the sun. No longer did long, darting shadows—his own and the handlers'—terrify the black. He let the boy stroke the white blaze on his forehead, a blaze so broad that it had given him his name of Oxhead—Bucephalus. Alexander vaulted on to his back, and the horse sprang away in mighty leaps. The struggle ended with Bucephalus galloping smoothly around the course, responding to his rider's every word and touch.

1

A soothsayer among the watching crowd called out: "Now can the oracle be fulfilled! It was foretold that when Alexander mastered a wild black horse, he would mount the throne of Macedon."

Before long, Philip lay dead beneath an assassin's knife, and his son and heir led an army across the Hellespont and southward on that extraordinary, years-long march which would end in his conquest of all the known world and gain for him the title Alexander the Great.

Always it was Bucephalus the King rode in combat, though lesser mounts served him for marches. While the spear-bristling Macedonian phalanx bored into the enemy's center, Alexander on his great black war horse launched the thundering cavalry charges that smashed in a flank. Darius and his host were routed on two hard-fought fields, and the mighty Persian Empire humbled in the dust. The rich cities of the Phœnicians fell, and the ancient land of Egypt bowed to the conqueror.

Once at a desert camp, Bucephalus was stolen by nomads. The furious Alexander sent warning he would scour the land with his entire army and leave no man alive, unless his beloved steed was restored. Trembling tribesmen hastened to return the horse.

Bucephalus grew old, as years of conflict hewed out the vast domain. He was eighteen, but still his master's favorite charger when Alexander rode him in the bloody battle that shattered the array of King Porus of India, and his armored elephants. In the midst of the fight, the black's aged heart gave

Paul Brown

way and, without a wound on his body, he dropped and died.

Alexander buried his gallant horse with ceremony in a splendid tomb of alabaster tiles, adorned with gold leaf, on the banks of the Hydaspes River and there in his honor founded a city named Bucephala.

A tale declares that the great war horse's fame was also carried on for a time by his descendants. Marco Polo, in his journey through the East in the early fourteenth century, visited the province of Balaxiam in Tartary and wrote: "The Countrey itselfe is very cold. It hath many Horses, and those excellent, great, and swift, which have so hard and strong hoofes on their feet that they need no Iron Shoes, although they runne through Rockes. It is said that not long since there were Horses of the Race of Alexander's Bucephalus, all with his forehead-marke, in the possession of the Kings Uncle, who was slaine for denying the King to have them: whereupon his Widow in angry spite destroyed the whole Race."

CAESAR'S HORSE

THROW-BACK TO EOHIPPUS

SOOTHSAYERS watched the young Roman general breaking the colt he himself had bred. The horse was as wild as he was strong, and the struggle between him and his rider was long and exhausting. In spite of his rearing and kicking, the colt gradually was brought under control, for the man on his back was a consummate horseman. As the battle between wills came to an end, and the lathered animal obeyed the commands of reins and legs, the admiring soothsayers advanced and uttered a prediction:

"As you have mastered this horse, Caius Julius Cæsar, so will you one day gain mastery over the world."

They ran no great risk with their prophecy. Already Cæsar had won his reputation as Rome's foremost military leader and he held the highest political offices of the Republic. With his limitless, unscrupulous ambition, it was indeed safe to predict he would rise to the summit of power.

Every sight of Cæsar's horsemanship reminded men of the soothsayers' words. An expert rider from childhood, he would drop his reins and gallop at full speed with his arms clasped

5

behind his back, or wield sword and javelin with perfection. No other could mount the horse he had trained and sat with such tireless ease.

Besides his swiftness and strength, Cæsar's horse possessed an extraordinary feature. All his hoofs were divided so that they resembled toes. Thus he was a throw-back to the prehistoric ancestor of the horse, *eohippus,* whose feet, split into toes, four on the forefeet and three on the hindfeet, later developed into solid hoofs.

Horses always stood high among Cæsar's interests. In addition to the bloody combats of gladiators and wild beasts which furthered his political fortunes with the Romans, he staged frequent riding and chariot races in the Circus Maximus. He revived the Trojan Games in which mounted troops of young noblemen engaged in mock combats which required the most accomplished horsemanship.

In campaigns described in his *Commentaries,* Cæsar rode his toed steed. From the saddle he dictated to three or more mounted secretaries. For the long, rapid journeys he made— sometimes as far as one hundred miles a day—he spared himself and his horse by shifting to a light carriage. When his steed was brought to him to lead a charge, he was likely to dismount and head the assault on foot to inspire his legions. "When I have won this battle," he would call out, "I will use my horse for the chase, but at present let us go against the enemy." And it was his practice when the issue of a battle seemed doubtful to send all horses, including his own, to the

Paul Brown

rear, so that his troops must stand their ground with no opportunity for flight.

Some years before Cæsar fell beneath the daggers of assassins, his horse died. Cæsar caused a statue of the celebrated animal to be made and placed before the temple of Venus.

THE SEIAN HORSE

BAD LUCK ON HIS BACK

IT was true that the horse which belonged to Cneius Seius descended from ill-omened forebears. He was of the Argive breed, stemming from the mares of Diomed—ferocious, man-eating creatures. Barbarous Diomed had fed his enemies and sacrificial victims to them, until Hercules, performing his eighth labor, tossed the king to his own mares to devour. Loosed on Mount Olympus, the mares themselves were destroyed by wolves or other wild beasts.

Such old tales disturbed Cneius Seius not at all. His steed was a beauty—a bay, some say, others a sorrel, with a full, shining mane and tail. More probably he was a dun like most of the Argive strain; today we might describe him as a buckskin or palomino. And he was of extraordinary size, which made him a valuable asset in the consulship of Julius Cæsar when conflicts constantly flamed up at home and abroad, and a Roman knight had need of a large, strong war horse.

The great stature of the Seian horse drew further mutterings from the superstitious. They declared he reminded them of the huge wooden horse which the Greeks, concealing warriors

9

in his belly, had tricked the Trojans into dragging within their walls and so captured the city. Surely the big dun would bring ruin on any who took possession of him, just as had the Trojan horse.

Before long, the augurs of disaster were shaking their heads in gloomy satisfaction. Cneius Seius fell out with Mark Antony and was put to a cruel death by that powerful general.

A mere coincidence undoubtedly. Thus must have reasoned Cornelius Dolabella. Greatly admiring the dun, he bought him for 100,000 sesterces—and shortly was killed while fighting in the civil wars in Syria.

Caius Cassius, one of the leading conspirators who had stabbed Cæsar to death in the Senate, next acquired the Seian horse. Defeated at the Battle of Philippi, Cassius preferred suicide to execution and fell on his own sword.

The chain of fateful events linked in full circle when Mark Antony, slayer of Seius, became the horse's next master. Dallying overlong with Cleopatra in Egypt, the general finally mustered an army and fleet to face Octavius, the future Augustus Cæsar. Conquered at Actium, Antony fled to perish in a death pact with the Egyptian queen.

Historians do not state whether any other man ever dared own the ominous animal, and the dun himself disappears from their pages. Yet he left behind him a Latin proverb. Of anyone who met with a series of misfortunes it was long said: *"Ille homo habet equum Seianum"*—"That man has a Seian horse."

INCITATUS

NEARLY A ROMAN CONSUL

INCITATUS *bids you to a banquet at his house.*

Thus, graven on waxen tablets delivered by imperial messengers, read the invitations. Dignified Roman senators stifled their emotions and hastened to accept. It did not matter that they had been asked to dine with a horse. Incitatus was the favorite steed of the Emperor Caligula, and to decline would be risking death by slow torture.

Caligula, son of the great soldier, Germanicus, had succeeded Tiberius on the throne of the Cæsars. His early rule was mild and benevolent. Then, following a severe illness, he turned into one of the most vicious tyrants the world has ever known. No man or woman, however honored and exalted, was safe from his cruelty and lust. Thousands were murdered at his whim, or sent to the arena to perish in combats with gladiators or wild beasts. No wonder Romans never dared refuse his horse's invitations.

Incitatus, a splendid animal whose very name expressed the swiftness with which he answered the spur, received his guests

Paul Brown

in his domicile, elegantly furnished and staffed by a troop of slaves. Draped in a purple blanket, a collar of precious gems about his neck, the equine host stood in a stall of marble. The Emperor himself saw to it that Incitatus' ivory manger was filled with the finest grain and he drank his steed's health in wine from golden goblets.

If Caligula had a redeeming feature, it was his fondness for horses. He appeared at his best astride Incitatus or driving in chariot races. At times with fiendish glee he forced senators, clad in their voluminous togas, to run for miles beside his chariot. The Emperor was an ardent partisan of the Green faction of charioteers. He spent many a night carousing with them in their stables and bet huge sums on them when they competed on the course, constructed on the site of an aqueduct which he had destroyed for that purpose. To make the track more spectacular, he caused it to be strewn with vermilion. Woe betide the Blues, Whites, or Reds when they won! Caligula sometimes ordered their drivers poisoned and, forgetting his love for horses, their teams as well.

Always he heaped honors on Incitatus. He made the horse a priest. Finally the Emperor announced that he was about to appoint his mount to the highest office in the land after his own. Before he could act, retribution for his crimes caught the tyrant. In 41 A.D. a tribune of the guard drew his sword and stabbed Caligula. But for that, Incitatus would have become a consul of the Roman Empire.

BROIEFORT

TROPHY FROM THE SARACENS

OGIER the Dane, fighting for the Emperor Charlemagne, joined combat with a gigantic Moorish king. Every blow he dealt carefully, so as not to harm the splendid steed ridden by his adversary. The Dane's shout soared above the clash of arms:

"I would rather have that horse than aught else that now is or ever has been!"

At length he smote the Saracen senseless from his saddle and gained the black Arabian charger he coveted. Broiefort's beauty equaled his strength. A white new moon marked his ebony forehead, and his forefeet were white also. So close became the bond between horse and master that all the paladins declared that it would be as strange to see a sword without its hilt as Ogier without Broiefort.

In many a fray, Ogier, mounted on the black, fought valiantly for Charlemagne, who had taken him as hostage from his father, the King of Denmark. Once he saved the Emperor's life. But a scoundrelly son of Charlemagne, angered at defeat in a chess game by Ogier's son, slew the youth with the board.

Ogier, balked in an attempt to take vengeance, was forced to flee to Lombardy. When Charlemagne demanded his return in chains, the Lombard ruler refused, and war was declared. In the ensuing battle, Ogier's armor was hewn from him and he was wounded by seven spear thrusts. Unhorsed, forced to one knee, his sword broken, he was going down before the Frankish onslaught, when Broiefort galloped to his rescue. The black Arabian killed two squires and five horses with his hoofs and routed a whole company of men-at-arms. His master remounted and cut his way out of the melee.

Ogier outdistanced hot pursuit. That evening the exhausted knight halted and fell into a deep slumber. When Broiefort heard oncoming foemen, he neighed and stamped, but could not arouse the sleeper. Finally he seized Ogier by the collar and dragged him to his feet, only just in time for escape.

But on another occasion the two were surprised and captured. Ogier was cast into a dungeon and would have been put to death by the implacable Charlemagne, had not all the knights of the realm interceded for him. Because Broiefort threw the captor who tried to ride him, the steed was turned over to a carter and condemned to haul stones the rest of his life.

For seven years the Danish paladin languished in a Rheims prison, while his charger toiled at his ignominious task. Then a formidable attack by the King of Mauretania imperiled the Empire. The people demanded Ogier's release, and Charlemagne complied. Despite his long imprisonment, the Dane was still a mighty man. No horse could bear his weight. At length

Paul Brown

someone remembered the cart nag, and Broiefort was brought. One glimpse of his master, and the old war horse's spirit revived. He stamped in delight, whinnied and placed his black muzzle in Ogier's hands.

Ogier rode him in the battle on which hung the fate of France. All day it raged, with neither side prevailing. As night fell, Ogier charged down on the Saracen sovereign. Never had he encountered so fierce a foe. At the height of their desperate duel, the pagan treacherously swept his scimitar down on Broiefort's neck. Ogier, his mount sinking under him, ran the king through. The victory was won, but the gallant black charger was dead.

BABIECA

STEED OF EL CID

LEGEND declares that Ruy Diaz de Bivár captured his steed in battle. That national hero of Spain, called El Cid—Arabic for the lord—waged many wars in the last half of the eleventh century, defending his native land against the Moors who had invaded from North Africa. But a likelier tale of how he came to own the charger, which he rode all his life and whose fame is coupled with his, runs otherwise, and the horse's strange name confirms it.

In his youth, Ruy Diaz begged his godfather, a priest of Burgos, for the gift of a colt. The priest offered him his pick from a paddock full of mares with their foals. After shrewd study, the lad selected an ugly, mangy colt. His godfather smilingly chided him:

"Babieca [booby, in the Spanish tongue], thou hast chosen ill."

Unswerving, the boy repeated the taunt. "Babieca—that will be a good name for my horse."

Surface looks had not deceived the young horseman's eyes. Under careful tending the dirty, scabrous hide became a coat of snowy white. Babieca, true to his Arab or Barb breeding, proved his fleetness and courage, as his master won his spurs and his title as El Cid in fierce combat with the Saracens. Ruy Diaz was a champion of the realm when it struck him that none less than royalty should ride so splendid a steed as his. He journeyed to the court of King Alfonso to put Babieca through his paces. In a matchless display of horsemanship and training, a rein broke but the white charger readily answered the pressure of his rider's legs. To a loyal proffer of the horse, the King replied that he would accept him in token but that El Cid must keep him to perform astride him those feats of arms which had honored Spain and all Christendom.

The paladin and Babieca did valiant service until El Cid died in the defense of Valencia, hotly besieged by a vast Moorish army. All sign of mourning was suppressed. That night the hero's embalmed body was dressed in armor, his head encased in a helmet of gilt parchment, his shield hung around his neck, his sword fastened in his hand, and his black beard bound as was his custom with a cord beneath his breastplate. Then the dead man was braced in Babieca's saddle.

With six hundred horsemen before and a like number behind Babieca and his ghostly burden, the garrison rode forth in a desperate sally and fell on the Moorish host. Babieca charged into the thick of the fray. As always the sight of the redoubtable champion on his white steed wrought havoc among the foe. Ten thousand fleeing Moors were drowned in the sea, and the rest embarked on ships.

Babieca lived two and one-half years longer, dying at the hoary age of forty. They buried him deep, as El Cid had bade. "When ye bury Babieca, dig deep, for it were a shameful thing that he who hath trampled down so many dogs of Moors, should be eaten by curs." Two elms were planted before the gate of the Monastery of San Pedro de Careña to mark the grave.

SHARATZ

A VISION STORMED A CASTLE

SHARATZ was a piebald or pinto stallion. His varicolored hide, later a favorite with the North American Indians, was strange indeed for the steed of a fourteenth-century Balkan paladin. Old ballads of Serbia declare the marking was caused by leprosy, of which Sharatz was cured when a colt, by his master, Prince Marko Kralyevitch.

Those epic ballads, still sung by the Serbs today, celebrate the mighty deeds of Marko and Sharatz. Of such strength and size was the piebald, he was the only horse the Prince could not swing by the tail. His master taught him to drink wine and always carried a wine-skin, slung to his saddle, for their refreshment. Sharatz mounted guard while Marko slept. In battle he was terrible. He would smite the horses of the enemy and sever their ears from their heads with his gleaming teeth, while trampling Turkish warriors to death. When a foeman aimed a sudden and unexpected lance thrust at his master, the charger would kneel to let it pass harmlessly above. Rider and horse are exalted in the ballads as "a dragon mounted upon a dragon."

But beneath the glamour of folklore, history reveals Prince Marko as a patriot and valiant fighter, and Sharatz as a steed worthy of him. The Prince's gallant defense of Serbia against the power of the Turkish Empire should have won him the kingship. When an opposing faction cheated him of the election, he went over for a time to the enemy. Yet his countrymen forgave him and after his death in the Battle of Rovina in 1399, he was enshrined as a national hero.

It is related that when Marko knew his end was near, he cut off the head of Sharatz and broke his sword and lance rather than allow prized possessions to fall into the hands of the Turks. Master and steed were buried in a cavern in Mount Urvine, frowning down on the Castle of Prilip. There they sleep through the centuries until their country's peril wakes them. Then Marko's sword rises from its sheath, embedded in the summit, Sharatz munches the last of his hay, and the twain gallop forth to do battle for Serbia once more.

How vividly they still live in the hearts of Serbs is strikingly demonstrated by an historic incident of the First World War. Again the mountain kingdom was invaded by her ancient antagonist, Turkey, ally of the Germans. Turkish colors floated over the Castle of Prilip, and the Serbs besieged its walls, bristling with cannon and machine guns and seemingly impregnable. One day Serbian troops suddenly sprang from their trenches and surged forward without orders. Frantic shouts by officers failed to stem the tide. Forward swept the assault, storming and taking the castle. Afterwards this explanation

Paul Brown

of their victory was given by soldiers, their eyes still alight with a vision.

"Prince Marko commanded us all the time, 'Forward!' Did you not see him on his Sharatz?"

JOAN OF ARC'S CHARGER

HE BORE A MAID IN ARMOR

JOAN OF ARC stood in a doorway opening on the town square of Orléans, newly relieved from English siege by the army of France she led. Scarcely healed was the arrow wound she had taken, valiantly heading the attack. Every eye in the array of French chivalry, spearmen, and bowmen mustered there was fixed on her bright and smiling face. Her look was rapt as when, a peasant girl in the village of Domrémy, she had hearkened to Voices bidding her save her country from the invader. The dark hair of her unhelmeted head was cut short like a soldier's, and the white armor she wore gleamed in the sunlight. One sturdy hand grasped a lance from which a pennant flaunted; the other a small battle ax as a badge of command.

A sudden commotion rose, and ranks opened hastily for the passage of a fiery black charger. The gift of the Dauphin Charles to the Maid, this sable stallion was a *destrier,* or Great Horse, forebear of the heavy draft animals of today. He would hardly feel the light burden he saw awaiting him. His mighty strength and stature were capable of carrying more than four hundred and twenty pounds, weight of a knight in chain mail and plate armor. As he was led forward for Joan to mount, he pawed the earth and snorted furiously. Dragging his crimson bridle from a groom's grasp, he reared aloft, wild, unmanageable.

The Maid's countenance remained calm. She knew horses, having cared for and ridden farm animals all her life. With a steady glance at the unruly steed, she ordered:

"Take him to the Cross there, before us, by the Church."

Bold spirits succeeded in seizing the bridle. Confronted by the holy emblem, so the story goes, the great stallion stood stockstill for Joan of Arc to mount to his saddle amid the cheers of knights and men-at-arms.

She rode him to Rheims for the triumphant coronation of Charles. He was her mount when she and Du Guesclin led the dashing cavalry raids that harassed the foemen from across the Channel. He carried her to the storming of Paris, held by the Burgundians and English, where, in spite of a second wound, the gallant girl urged on the assault till comrades forced her from the field. She bestrode him on that ill-starred day when, repulsed after a sally from Compiègne, she and a rearguard were holding off the enemy by desperate fighting when an archer dragged her from the saddle and took her prisoner.

The sable stallion would see her no more. Tried and condemned by a court convened by her merciless foes, the Maid was burned at the stake.

Paul Brown

MORZILLO

HORSE THAT BECAME A GOD

"FOR, after God, we owed the victory to our horses."

Thus, four centuries ago, wrote Bernal Diaz, chronicling one of the battles in which the Spanish Conquistadores wrested the empire of Mexico from Montezuma and his Aztec warriors. And chief among the steeds paid that tribute was the coal-black stallion, ridden by the leader, Cortez.

El Morzillo—"The Black One"—was one of the seventeen mounts aboard the little fleet sailing from Cuba in the first expedition to Mexico. His forebears were the fine animals, rich in the blood of Arabs and Barbs, shipped from Spain and bred in the Caribbean islands. From these stemmed the horses that would spread through the whole North American continent. When Cortez and his scanty cavalry thundered down on the Indian masses, the tribesmen fled in terror. Never had they beheld horses, fierce, fleet, snorting monsters, which must be gods or demons. No wonder the Spaniards, winning battle after battle, called their steeds their companions and their salvation.

Paul Brown

When the original mount of Cortez, a chestnut, was killed, he took "The Black One," jointly owned by a trumpeter and a trooper. On thrust the Conquistadores until Montezuma's capital, the present Mexico City, was stormed, and the Emperor taken captive and slain. Then came disaster, with the Spaniards themselves besieged. Cortez on Morzillo led a desperate retreat, fighting through overwhelming numbers. Sorely wounded by rocks and an arrow, the general slipped from the saddle. At that moment, a feathered shaft struck Morzillo in the mouth. The big black, maddened by anger and pain, sprang at the encircling Aztecs, biting and striking with his hoofs. When Cortez managed to mount again, he launched a charge that carried the day, and finally the city was recaptured.

Cortez rode the black when he marched to Honduras in 1524 to quell a lieutenant's rebellion. Emerging from jungles, the column entered a valley where a Mayan tribe tended sacred deer. These the Spaniards hunted, firing from horseback. The spectacle of strange creatures, fire spouting from their backs, drove the panicky Indians to surrender. But Morzillo ran a splinter deeply into one foot, and Cortez was forced to leave him with the Mayans. "See you take the best of care of him," the Conquistador growled through his bristling, black beard. "If my beloved steed is not here when I return——" He had no need to finish the threat.

The frightened Mayans obeyed. Installing Morzillo in the largest temple of their lake-island city, they worshiped him as the God of Thunder and Lightning. Maidens wreathed his neck with flowers, and he was fed chickens and other delicacies. When the black horse died, either from grief for a master who never came for him or the odd diet, the tribe carved a stone statue of him, seated on his haunches.

A century later, two Franciscans found the Mayans still bowing down before their horse idol. "This is no god but only the image of an unthinking beast!" the missionaries cried. One of the friars, risking martyrdom in his zeal, shattered the statue's head with a club.

Still El Morzillo is remembered in Mexico. Today native canoe men declare that on clear, moonless nights you can see in the depths of the lake the likeness of the horse that was worshiped as a god.

MAROCCO

HIS TRICKS WERE HIS SALVATION

MAROCCO could walk on his hind legs and dance. At the command of his master, a Scot named Banks, the medium-size bay would pick up articles in his teeth and carry them to persons indicated. His most amazing feat was reading the dots on dice and tapping out the number with a forefoot, shod in silver. So clever were Marocco's tricks, Shakespeare wrote of him in *Love's Labour's Lost:* "How easy it is to put years to the word three, and study three years in two words, the dancing horse will tell you."

There were few performing horses in that day, and Marocco's exhibitions drew crowds to the inn courts and lined the galleries with spectators. Banks, a good showman, would introduce such sure-fire acts as ordering Marocco to carry a glove to the most beautiful lady present or pick out the gentleman who was the greatest slave of the fair sex.

In 1600, to promote business, the Scot caused his horse to climb the stairs to the vane at the top of St. Paul's. Goggle-eyed throngs gathered, staring upward. Banks' publicity stunt fell flat with only one crabbed resident who, hastily summoned

Paul Brown

by his servant to witness the marvelous spectacle, growled crossly: "Away, you fool! Why need I go so far to see a horse on the top when I can see so many asses at the bottom?"

The showman took his celebrated performer on tour to Scotland and then to France. All went well until the word began to spread that Marocco's remarkable tricks were due to witchcraft. Banks made the rash mistake of encouraging the rumor. During a show, a hue and cry arose that Marocco was a familiar of the Devil. Angry voices demanded that both horse and master be sent to Rome and burned at the stake as sorcerers.

Such a fate might easily have been theirs in that superstitious age. The quick-thinking Scot whispered urgent instruction in his pupil's ear. Both their lives were saved when Marocco walked gravely up to a man wearing a cross on his hat, kneeled down and bowed before the symbol.

GODOLPHIN BARB

CHANCE AND A FOUNDATION SIRE

AN Englishman named Coke, strolling along the Rue de Rivoli in Paris one day in 1731 glanced casually at the nag pulling a gardener's cart. He stopped and stared. His eye for good horseflesh told him that yonder, hitched to a load of vegetables, walked a horse that any ruler of the Barbary States might proudly have ridden.

Surely that unkempt animal between the shafts was a Barb —one of those splendid steeds of Africa, famed even in the days of ancient Egypt. The winged Pegasus himself, so mythology declared, was foaled in the Libyan desert. Larger and somewhat more coarsely built than Arab horses, Barbs rivaled them in speed and endurance and were equally prized.

The Briton halted the driver with eager questions. How had he come into possession of that horse? Bought at the Port St. Denis market from an Arab, m'sieu. Ah, that explained much. One might purchase many things at the "Thieves' Market," and, asking no questions, frequently get a bargain. Was the horse for sale? But certainly, for a price. When the haggling was over, Coke owned the gardener's nag.

How the Barb had reached France and turned up at the
"Thieves' Market" is a mystery. Some say he had been a peace
offering from the Sultan of Morocco to Louis XIV, who was
angered by the Sultan's penchant for beheading Christians,
but the tale is doubtful. However that may be, after Coke
bought him he was sent to England, changed hands once more,
and was presented to the Earl of Godolphin.

That nobleman was little impressed. The dark bay stallion,
standing 14½ hands, was plainly of Barbary stock (though
chronicles would often mistakenly term him an Arabian), but
his crest was abnormally large and spoiled his proportions.
Godolphin judged him unworthy to be admitted to his stud.
By that decision, the Earl came close to robbing equine posterity
of an invaluable strain and his own name of renown.

Now chance for a second time played a part in the Barb's
career. The mare Roxana was to have been bred to Hobgoblin,
pride of Godolphin's stables. In a romantic novel, Eugene Sue
tells of a fierce combat between the lordly stallion and the Barb
for Roxana's favor. But, in fact, Hobgoblin refused to cover
the mare. It happened that the Barb broke loose and served
Roxana, much to the annoyance of the Earl.

The nobleman's chagrin at the accident disappeared when
the colt was foaled. Named Lath, he proved to be so fine an
animal that his sire was continued at stud and was thenceforth
known as the Godolphin Barb. He fathered many another
swift colt and filly, and their descendants were more notable
still. To none did he transmit his ungainly crest.

Paul Brown

"Blood will tell" is a true saying of horses. Scan the stud-books, carefully kept anciently in the Orient, in England for more than two and a half centuries, and elsewhere, and you cannot doubt it. The records of racing winners also bear testimony. Bright on their pages shines the line of the Godolphin Barb. It is an extraordinary fact that most of the great horses of the turf today trace back to him and two other steeds of the East: the Darley Arabian and Byerly Turk. Authorities predict that the blood of those three great Foundation Sires will a hundred years hence be found in the veins of almost all the best race-horses.

A black cat was the constant companion and playfellow of the Godolphin Barb for the latter part of his life. When he died in his twenty-ninth year, the cat stood guard on his body until men came to bury him. Following to the grave, the cat watched till the earth covered his friend, then vanished, later to be found in a hayloft dead, they said, of grief.

BLACK BESS

HIGHWAYMAN'S HORSE

"STAND and deliver!"

The command brought the stagecoach on the moonlit, English country road to a sudden halt. Reining tight his snorting, frightened four, the coachman on his box stared down into the muzzles of a pair of leveled pistols. Passengers, groaning over the approaching loss of purses and watches, peered out at the debonair figure on horseback blocking the way.

That was Dick Turpin. No trifling with him. Moonlight glimmered on the hilt of the sword at his side and on the silver ornaments of the bridle of his sleek black mare. Collecting his plunder, the highwayman sped away with a clatter of hoofs. It would be vain to give the alarm at the next stage. Nobody could overtake Turpin on Black Bess.

Stolen with her foal by Turpin, the mare was prized by the robber above all his booty. She was reputed to be the get of an Arabian and an English racer. A poet, speaking for her master, hymned her thus:

41

> From the West was her dam; from the East was her sire.
> From the one came her swiftness; the other, her fire.
> No peer of the realm better blood can possess
> Than flows in the veins of my bonny Black Bess.

Swiftly the mare galloped with Turpin from his Epping Forest haunts to rob coaches and horsemen on the broad highway and as swiftly bore him away, escaping all pursuit. Black Bess could not understand she was serving a criminal, a former butcher's boy, who had stained his hands with human blood by the murder of a gamekeeper and the accidental shooting of a brother highwayman; a brutal desperado, who did not stop at torturing women on lonely farms to make them reveal hidden valuables. The mare knew only that she was loved and cared for tenderly. She regarded Dick Turpin as fondly as the hero-worshiping ostlers at inns, who aided and abetted him.

Black Bess came to share the glamour with which romancers covered her master. To the pair was credited the famous Ride to York, made by another highwayman on another mount some years after Turpin's death. They were celebrated in dramas, serials, and "penny dreadfuls"—dime novels. A book entitled *Black Bess; or the Knight of the Road, A Romance* sold two and one-half million copies. Dickens gave his "Sam Weller" this chorus to roar out with cronies over their cups:

> Dick Turpin once, on Hounslow Heath,
> His bold mare Bess bestrode-er,
> Whenas he sees the Bishop's coach
> A-coming along the road-er.

So he gallops up to the horses' heads,
And he claps his head within,
And the Bishop says, "Sure as eggs is eggs,
This here's the bold Tur*pin!*"

At last Black Bess in a way carried her master to the gallows. When he was caught and hanged at York in 1739, the charge on which Turpin was convicted was—stealing a black mare and foal.

ECLIPSE (English)

TEMPER AND A WHIRLWIND

AN eclipse blotted out the sun that day in 1764 when the little chestnut colt, with a white blaze from forehead to nose and a white off hind leg, was foaled in England. Superstitious stablemen saw an omen in the darkened skies and a name for the new colt. He was registered as Eclipse, and hopes were high that a great career on the turf lay before him. In his veins ran the blood of the Godolphin Barb and others of the swiftest steeds bred in the lands of High Barbary.

But expectations soon were dashed. Eclipse's fiery spirit and tremendous vitality vented themselves in an evil temper. He shied, bit, kicked and struck out viciously with his forefeet at men and other horses. His owner, despairing of bringing such an animal to the post, lent him to a poacher, who rode him hard through the forests night and day in all weather. A season of this bitter drudgery, and the stallion was ready to behave. He showed speed in trials and was sold at a good price to a heavy-gambling Irishman, Dennis O'Kelly.

Eclipse's new owner entered him in a small race, limited to five-year-olds which had never won. In the paddock, knowing squires sneered at the unpromising looks of the chestnut and offered big odds against him. O'Kelly grinned and took them. Bets dropped to even money. Again the Irishman covered, then gave odds himself until the cocked hats clutched by the stake-holders were heaped high with golden guineas.

Horses lined up at the post. The flag swept down, and they were off. O'Kelly's jubilant shout, a cry to be heard again on many a course, rang above the pounding hoofs:

"Eclipse first, and the rest nowhere!"

At the three-mile post, the field still was bunched. Then at the first lift of his jockey's whip, Eclipse forged out in front. He flashed over the green, seeming to cover twenty-five feet with every bound. So far did he outdistance the ruck, that his jockey pulled with all his might for the last mile in an attempt to prevent his mount's startling speed from being revealed. Eclipse could not be held. He crossed the finish line before the rest had turned the corner.

That same year, Eclipse won the King's Plate in five meets, along with other races. Odds on him began at 1 to 10, soared to 20, to 100. His jockeys never touched him with whip or spur nor tried again to rein him in. They simply sat their sad-dles, feeling as if they were flying, while the chestnut sprang into the lead. It mattered not the slightest that he customarily carried such heavy weight as 168 pounds. Always it was "Eclipse first, and the rest nowhere." He gained gold cups, silver plates, and purses galore for the beaming O'Kelly. After Eclipse's second season, nobody dared match a horse against

him, and he was retired and put to stud. Many of the fastest race-horses on record descended from him. He was the great-grandsire of the American Eclipse.

When this king of the English turf died at the age of twenty-six, he was given a royal funeral where cakes and ale were served, and O'Kelly hired a poet to write his epitaph.

RANGER

STUD WITH A LEGEND

FEW horses since Pegasus have been endowed with so wonderful a career as Ranger, sometimes called Lindsay's Arabian. Most of that gray stallion's past, as related in his stud advertisements, was as mythical as the tale of the winged steed of the Greeks, although Ranger's owners stopped short of claiming he could fly.

It is true that Ranger, bred in England, was imported to the American Colonies just before the Revolution. Probably some good Barb blood flowed in his veins, and certainly he served as a useful sire for some years in New England and the South. But there truth gives way to the following gorgeous legend, which spread through the States and was printed in many a book.

The tale runs that the captain of a British vessel, cruising the Mediterranean, once saved the life of a son of the Sultan of Morocco and was presented by the grateful potentate with a superb gray horse of the desert. Taking his gift aboard, the captain sailed west, put in at a Caribbean port and loosed the animal in a lumber yard for exercise. Ranger, dashing about in joy at being freed from confinement below decks, crashed into a pile of boards and broke three legs. His owner was about to order him destroyed, but was persuaded to give him to a Yankee shipmaster who declared, "I allow if I hed that critter aboard I could save him." Ranger, splinted and bandaged, was placed in a sling on the American ship. His broken bones had knitted by the time he was debarked at New London, Connecticut, and he was sold and put to stud. Some of his get became cavalry mounts in the Revolution and aroused the admiration of no less than General Washington, who ordered Lighthouse Harry Lee to buy the sire and send him to Virginia. Washington's famous gray coach horses and some of his stock at Mount Vernon were said to be descended from Ranger.

That romantic yarn was not spun until after a Captain Lindsay had bought Ranger and taken him to Maryland. For the benefit of owners of mares to be bred, the captain let his imagination work on Ranger's story. The stallion was renamed Lindsay's Arabian, which—like many so-called Arabians—he wasn't. A U. S. Supreme Court justice was said to have examined his legs and to have handed down a decision that one of them, anyway, once had been broken. Washington's favorite charger and the horse General Putnam rode down a flight of steps to escape British dragoons were stated to have been Ranger's colts. Every detail increased the demand for the gray's services.

Thus Ranger, legendary even in life, left hoofprints in the sands of time.

Paul Brown

MESSENGER

AMERICAN PATRIARCH

HORSES were scarce in the United States after the Revolution. Many had been killed in the campaigns, and mounts captured from the British did not begin to replace them. The great wild horse herds of the plains, ranging through Spanish and Indian lands, still were beyond our reach. On sturdy stock for transportation and farm work largely depended the growth of the young nation.

So it was something of an event when one day in 1788 a gray stallion, imported from England, charged down a packet's gangplank on to a Philadelphia wharf. Messenger had had his fill of being shut up in a hold. He plunged about, snorting through his trumpet-like nostrils, and grooms barely managed to cling to his halter rope. Onlookers were not impressed by his appearance. He was big—almost sixteen hands high—but ungainly. His record on the English turf was mediocre. Yet he combined the blood of all three of the Foundation Sires from the Orient, which had made English horseflesh great: the blood of the Godolphin Barb, the Darley Arabian, and the Byerly Turk. And he was a son of the celebrated Mambrino.

"In that horse, a million dollars steps on American soil," one spectator is supposed to have declared. Probably the remark was a postscript, shifted forward to a prophecy by a good story-teller. But it proved true.

Messenger soon was put to stud. Season after season he stood in various localities in the eastern seaboard states. The fiery stallion was sometimes hard to handle. Once, being ferried across the Delaware River, he reared and struck his groom with a new-shod hoof, killing him. But Messenger's feats as a sire and the quality of his progeny steadily increased his value. Several times in his career he changed hands, one of his owners being John Jacob Astor. The gray's services were leased for the then high fee of $1000 a season.

It did not take Messenger long to understand he was a celebrity. When he was led out, he would strike a proud and commanding attitude. As a sire he was sure and one of the most prolific ones on record. In one season he covered 126 mares. Since he was kept at stud on into his old age and did not die until 1808, the debt of the United States to Messenger for increasing its equine population was considerable. Nor was it a question of mere quantity. The sons and daughters of the big gray, which had won only three races out of eight himself, became great running race-horses. Their get, by a strange quirk, developed into a strain that dominated the world's harness tracks. Messenger is rated the foundation sire of all the trotting, pacing and gaited horses in America.

The grand old patriarch died on Long Island in 1808 at

the age of twenty-eight. All the countryside gathered for his burial under a big chestnut tree in front of his owner's home. Platoon volleys were fired over his grave as no less than his due.

Passing generations cherished his memory. When the tree fell, a marker was set up. Some years later, the noted Piping Rock golf club, established on the estate, assembled a large concourse of people at the grave and unveiled a bronze tablet on a granite boulder in honor of the mighty stallion.

JUSTIN MORGAN

"GREATEST LITTLE HORSE IN THE WORLD"

THEY hitched the chunky little bay to the log, a hefty pine stick larger horses had vainly struggled to drag through the Vermont woods down to the sawmill. A gallon of rum, wagered in the tavern yonder, said he couldn't haul it to the logway in three pulls. The bay's owner grinned confidently and invited three of the company to straddle the log for a ride.

"Watch your feet," the driver yelled. "When this colt gets apullin', something's got to come!"

A word, and the stocky stallion put his weight into the collar, willing as always, though he'd been working hard all day. His mighty chest and thigh muscles flexed and corded. He plunged ahead, bent so far forward he seemed to be crawling on his knees. Before he halted, he'd hauled the log and its riders halfway to the mark. Another lusty tug, and he made it, with one pull to spare.

That was Justin Morgan, foaled in 1789, named for the schoolteacher and singing-master who grudgingly took him in settlement of a debt of twenty-five dollars—and never made a

Paul
Brown

better bargain. A runt of a horse, not much over fourteen hands and under a thousand pounds, he not only won drawing matches but races, running, trotting and walking, all over the State. New Yorkers brought up a speedy roan to run against him, and when Justin Morgan was brought to scratch jeered: "Say, you forgot the plow!" But the roan ate dust, and the Yorkers went home with empty pockets.

At once spirited and gentle, the Morgan horse was in constant demand. Officers borrowed him to ride prancing in parades. Girls begged for him to carry them to dances and not a single party-goer in her best frock was chucked off in a mud puddle. Every season the schoolmaster put him to stud for a one- or two-dollar fee, advertising that "he is exceeding sure and gets curious colts." They were unusual, for the bay had been sired by a thoroughbred, captured from a Tory colonel during the Revolution. More curious still was the fact that the little stallion's descendants were destined to gallop through American history.

The schoolmaster died of lung-sickness, never suspecting his horse would make his name immortal. Once more Justin Morgan was sold for debt. Again and again he changed hands. One hard owner nearly killed him, driving him through heavy snows in a freight team. Yet, toiling and begetting, he survived till 1821, when at the ripe old age of thirty-two he died from another horse's kick.

He lives in his progeny. No other creature has possessed such extraordinary power to transmit his best characteristics so faithfully. Generation after generation and through all crosses, the fine Morgan traits persist. Turn the pages of American annals and you will find such glimpses as these:

Trotting races being won by the beautiful and never-beaten Black Hawk, grandson of Justin . . . a Morgan pulling a doctor's buggy through a snowstorm, never looking back but always facing the blast . . . Rienzi, a Morgan, carrying General Sheridan to save the day "from Winchester twenty miles away" . . . Morgans as favorite mounts for our cavalry in four wars . . . Morgans pulling Concord wagons westward— as cow horses—police mounts . . . imported by foreign countries to improve native stock . . . winning blue ribbons in fairs, horse shows, endurance rides.

Plaques in various New England villages commemorate Justin Morgan. A life-size bronze statue of him stands on the U. S. Department of Agriculture farm, Weybridge, Vermont, devoted to breeding Morgan horses. In 1939, Iowa celebrated the 150th anniversary of his birth with a horse show, and the Vermont legislature passed a resolution honoring "the greatest little horse in the world." That legislative body also published his history, adding to scores of books and articles about him, and topped it off with: "Vermont is famous for men, women, maple sugar, and Morgan horses."

> "The first are strong, the latter fleet,
> The second and third are exceedingly sweet,
> And all are uncommonly hard to beat."

LISETTE

MARBOT'S FIGHTING MARE

YOUNG Baron de Marbot, dashing cavalry captain in Napoleon's Grand Army, needed a remount. In 1805 he bought the mare, Lisette, a beautiful creature, light as a feather on her feet and usually so docile a child could ride her. But too often the mare displayed fits of vicious temper. She would seize a man she disliked in her strong teeth and hang on like a bulldog; it took four or five troopers to rescue her victim. Blindfolded and hobbled, she was saddled and bridled, and Marbot swung astride her. "Once on her back, she was a truly incomparable mount," he insisted.

Nevertheless, a horse with such a bad habit could not be used on a campaign. Marbot was regretfully preparing to dispose of the mare when his shrewd groom found a cure. One day when Lisette was in one of her worst moods, the groom approached with a scorching hot roast of meat. Snorting, Lisette sunk her teeth in it, squealed with pain as she burned her mouth and dropped the roast hastily. After that she was a model charger.

Soon she learned to hate the enemy. At the Battle of Jena,

60

Marbot captured a German Hussar officer, took his parole and courteously returned his saber. The second the hilt was in his grasp, the treacherous German cut Lisette across the shoulder, spurred his horse against her to bowl Marbot from the saddle and made his escape.

Another bitter experience awaited the mare on the snow-covered field of Eylau. Volunteering to carry a message to a surrounded French regiment, Marbot, saber drawn, galloped down on masses of Cossacks. The swift Lisette, skimming ditches like a swallow, darted past thousands of the foe and brought her master through unharmed. But the encircled regiment could not cut its way out, and its commander, determined to die rather than surrender, ordered Marbot to save the colors.

The captain mounted and rode hard. A bullet creased his scalp, covering him with blood. Russian infantry closed in from all sides with muskets flaming. As an officer's sword pierced Marbot, a bearded grenadier sprang forward and plunged his bayonet into Lisette's chest. Even in the midst of the melee, Marbot shuddered at the sight he then beheld. Lisette screamed with fury, bared her teeth and bit off the entire face of the grenadier.

Then the mare killed the officer who had wounded her master. With gnashing, gory jays and flailing hoofs, she fought her way through the Russians and, while Marbot clung weakly to the saddle, galloped clear.

Racing toward the French ranks, Marbot was mistaken for an enemy officer leading a charge. A battalion of the Old

Guard gave him a volley. Lead riddled his cloak but he rode on till Lisette, faint from loss of blood, crashed down, and her rider was flung senseless in the snow.

The tide of battle swept over him. When he recovered consciousness, he saw Lisette standing protectingly beside him. Cold had congealed the mare's bleeding wound, and she had staggered to her feet and regained some strength by eating straw from soldiers' bedding. Then she had returned and stayed faithfully by her master's side until his searching orderly found them.

Recovering, the two served on through another campaign, during which Lisette was worn down by hard service. Marbot could ask no more of her. He retired her to the estate of a friend whose wife rode the mare for some years until her death from old age. Marbot fought on through the wars on other mounts, but Lisette he never forgot. His fighting mare gallops with him through the stirring pages of his memoirs.

COPENHAGEN

WELLINGTON'S WAR HORSE

ASTRIDE his powerful, red-gold chestnut, the Duke of Wellington galloped in the forefront of his battles against Napoleon's marshals in Spain. Once he rallied the British infantry, with an advancing French column only twenty yards away. Where the Iron Duke led, victory followed. Shot and shell daunted neither him nor his charger.

In Copenhagen breathed the spirit of the war horse of the Book of Job. "He goeth on to meet the armed men. He mocketh at fear, and is not affrighted; neither turneth he back from the sword." The chestnut carried the British commander through all hazards and weather of the damp, tough Peninsular campaign. The Duke suffered from rheumatism, but not so his mount, which seemed to move on steel springs.

Wellington had acquired the horse from a brother officer at the siege of Copenhagen in 1807 and named him for the captured Danish capital. The chestnut stallion was a grandson of the great English racer, Eclipse. Though his dam was a half-bred hunting mare, his master proudly termed him "much more thoroughly bred than most of the men I know."

Paul Brown

On the desperately fought field of Waterloo, scarlet ranks cheered to an echo, as the Iron Duke on Copenhagen thundered up into the hottest part of the fray. British squares, which had held firm against every assault of the French cavalry, bent back, keeping a safe distance from Copenhagen's flashing heels, when the Duke rode close to give praise. At the battle's crisis, Wellington himself launched the smashing infantry attack that shattered the last charge of Napoleon's Old Guard. Sabers flashing, British and Prussian horsemen completed the rout, and the pale Emperor fled, conquered at last.

The weary Wellington rode back over the battlefield where within three square miles were strewn 45,000 dead and wounded. Smoke-grimed and exhausted after eighteen hours in the saddle, he stiffly dismounted. Copenhagen, still fresh and lively, lashed out with an affectionate kick that nearly brained his master.

During the years the hero of Waterloo served his country as a leading statesman, the close comradeship between him and his steed never failed. Artists often painted Copenhagen and offered the portraits to his owner. The Duke sighed and bought them all, good or bad. As a mark of special favor, he let ladies ride the charger, now tamed by age. But one belle, enjoying the treat of a ride, was given some frightened moments when trumpets sounded in the distance. As in the old days, the old war horse snorted and pawed the ground. Then he took the bit in his teeth, dashed off at a headlong gallop and plunged with the fair rider straight into the center of a regiment forming a square. "Take care of that 'ere horse," warned a voice from the ranks. "He kicks out. We knew him in Spain."

When Copenhagen died in 1836, he was buried under an oak, with a headstone inscribed to him, on the Wellington estate. His master to the last day of his own life delighted in relating fond memories of his charger's deeds. Today a statue of Wellington, mounted on Copenhagen, stands atop Constitution Hill in London, a statue cast from captured cannon, fitting metal for the Iron Duke and his iron horse.

MARENGO

NAPOLEON'S FAVORITE

T HOROUGH and severe was the training given Marengo and the other Arabians and Barbs, mostly whites and grays, at the Imperial stud farm at St. Cloud, for they must be fitted to serve as chargers of the Emperor of the French, Napoleon Bonaparte. They were made accustomed to gunfire since they would be ridden through the din of mighty battles. They were taught not to shy when dogs and pigs were driven between their legs. Armand Caulaincourt, Master of the Horse, who rode behind the Emperor in combat, prepared to surrender his own mount to Napoleon in case of need, supervised the schooling. Jardin, head groom, saw to it that each horse was gentled and easy-gaited.

The cream-white stallion Marengo, named after the victory in which a French cavalry charge carried the day, was conspicuous among the fifty fine horses of the stud. He may have been one of the ten steeds presented to Napoleon by the Bey of Tunis, courting the favor of France against England.

No wonder that Marengo became the Emperor's favorite. His splendid looks set off the short, gray-coated figure astride

him. Under musketry and heavy cannonade, he stood unflinching and took wounds like a soldier. His endurance was proof
against the demands of a rider who sometimes wore out three
horses a day. More important, he was docile and sure-footed,
as he had need to be. The great Napoleon was no great horseman. He rode loosely, using his legs little, and he was given
to reining in suddenly and to galloping down steep slopes.
Though no one dared mention it, the Emperor took more than
a few falls.

At the Battle of Austerlitz, Marengo's speed saved Napoleon from a sudden rush by hard-riding Cossacks which came
within an ace of capturing him. The desert-bred steed served
through the Russian campaign and gallantly endured the terrible retreat from Moscow through snow and bitter cold. He
was among the eight horses taken to Elba when the victorious
Allies exiled Napoleon to that island. Marengo shared his
master's escape and return to France where armies rallied again
to his standard, and Europe was plunged once more into war.

It was at Waterloo that Marengo received his seventh
wound in action. He saw waves of French cavalry dash, break
and ebb back from the steady British squares. Perhaps his flashing eyes caught sight of a rival war horse, Copenhagen, with
Wellington on his back. As the British Guards charged and
Blücher's Prussians closed in, Napoleon attempted to flee but
was taken and imprisoned on the island of St. Helena, where
he ended his days.

This time Marengo was not permitted to accompany his

master. He was bought by a Frenchman, who sent him to an English estate, where the white charger died in 1829.

Living, Marengo had carried Great Britain's most formidable foe, whose defeat had cost years of conflict, many lives, and utmost resources. Dead, the charger's remains became a trophy. His skeleton was placed in a London museum. One of his hoofs, made into a snuffbox, is a memento in the mess of the Brigade of Guards.

TRUXTON

DEBT AND A DUEL

IT was a big price Andrew Jackson paid for that Virginia horse. Fifteen hundred dollars, part cash and part a swap of three geldings, with a promised bonus of three more, if the seventeen-hand bay stallion with white hind feet won the race planned for the spring. But the bay was a beautifully formed animal, and where good horseflesh was involved, Andy Jackson forgot the caution proper to a leading Tennessee lawyer and planter. He named his new racer after Commodore Truxton, Amercian naval hero. Most called the horse Truxton; his master's pet name for him was "The Commodore."

Truxton was carefully trained. A great deal depended on his winning the coming race in which he was matched against the noted Greyhound, which previously had beaten him. Yet that defeat had been due to poor conditioning, Jackson believed. He readily subscribed his share of the $5000 stake and allowed his wife and niece to wager their own saddle horses. Although Greyhound was the heavy favorite, he rashly plunged further

PAUL BROWN

and literally "bet his shirt," putting up $1500 worth of wearing apparel.

A great deal indeed hung on Truxton's victory. His owner's resources were strained to the limit. General Andrew Jackson, future conqueror of the British at New Orleans and President of the United States, was close to going to jail for debt.

Before the jockey mounted up for the race, the General spoke to his horse, as his custom was. He stroked Truxton's nose and looked him straight in the eye. Men swore Old Hickory had a way of implanting in a horse his own indomitable will to win.

Nobly the big bay responded. He sped over the track like lightning, and Greyhound ate his dust. From that day forth, his winnings and stud fees swelled the Jackson fortunes, while he and his progeny made their owner the leading figure of the American turf.

Another match for Truxton came close to setting his master's feet on the path to the grave. "The Commodore" was to meet a fast horse named Ploughboy, when the latter went lame, and his owner paid a forfeit. The next time the race was scheduled, Truxton in his turn was lame. Nevertheless, Jackson confidently ran him, and the bay overcame his stiffness to win a couple of two-mile heats. But rivalry had heated the hot blood of the frontier. The son-in-law of Ploughboy's owner, Charles Dickinson, smarting under defeat, made disparaging remarks about Jackson's marriage. Andrew and his Rachel had married in the mistaken belief that her divorce from her first husband had become final. Although they repeated the ceremony when they learned of the error, Jackson's enemies descended to spreading slander. When Dickinson did so, Jackson challenged him.

Few thought General Jackson would return to race Truxton again the morning he rode out to face a deadly duelist. Dickinson, reputed the best shot in Tennessee, fired first. Old Hickory stood firm under the impact of a bullet that broke a rib. He raised his own pistol, took steady aim and fired. His antagonist fell, mortally wounded.

Truxton, an underlying cause of a quarrel which had almost cost the United States a great soldier and President, continued his triumphant career on the turf and at stud, begetting four hundred sons and daughters. Jackson would visit him every night in his stall before retiring. When the press of national affairs prevented the General from giving his personal attention to training, he sold his racing stables. Truxton he could not bear to sell. He gave him to a friend in Mississippi, where the bay ended his days.

ECLIPSE (American)

HE CARRIED THE NORTH'S COLORS

"ECLIPSE against the world?"

Men of the Northern States, bound for the great race on Long Island's Union course that May day in 1824, shouted their boast back and forth. It ran along the eight miles, solid with carriages and horsemen, crawling from New York City, a line that was a preview of the automobile traffic jams of a century later. Angry arguments burst out when sudden stops drove the poles of a dozen vehicles through rear panels of rigs ahead.

"Eclipse against the world!" The boast was not as high-flown as it sounded. The North had defied the South to find a horse able to beat Eclipse, grandson of Diomed, English Derby winner of 1780. Southerners, who might have imported a foreign racer, had preferred to pick North Carolina's Sir Henry, also descended from Diomed. Cousin was matched against cousin.

Sixty thousand spectators filled the stands, lined the track and perched in trees. Wagers on the race and on its three grueling four-mile heats soared to $200,000. Northerners backed

76

Paul Brown

their favorite heavily, and the men from the South covered their bets, shrewd planters putting most of their money on the first heat.

Saddled up, the contenders showed their relationship. Both were dark sorrels with white markings. Sir Henry was a little smaller but five years younger. Eclipse, though nine, was still in his prime and a veteran race-horse. Yet Northerners were worried that Purdy, Eclipse's regular jockey, had fallen out with the horse's owner and was not scheduled to ride.

The two sleek sorrels were brought to the post, John Walden in sky-blue silks up on Sir Henry, and Eclipse with William Crofts in crimson on his back. Tense partisans held their breath.

A sharp tap on the starter's drum and they were off. Eclipse had drawn the pole, but he was poorly ridden and he tired. Sir Henry forged ahead and won the heat to the wild and jubilant whooping of the South.

Before the second heat, a stir of excitement spread from the paddock through the course. A small, gray-haired figure strode in, stripped off outer clothes to reveal racing silks and was given a leg up on Eclipse. Sam Purdy had changed his mind.

Eclipse, under the expert Purdy's guidance, stole the rail. On the turns he swung wide and forced his opponent out. Sir Henry gamely drew up to his girth, but the older sorrel won by two lengths. One heat apiece now.

Frantic cheering sped the racers around the course in the

decisive third. Eclipse thundered into the lead. Purdy and Taylor, now up on Sir Henry, rode hard, whipping and spurring mercilessly until their mounts bled. The Southern sorrel was staggering on the last lap but challenged until he was almost neck and neck. Eclipse, exhausted too, called on his last reserve, opened daylight between them and crossed the finish line a winner.

Eclipse, aged thirty-four, died in **1847**. Soon the race tracks he knew would empty into battlefields, and riders don the Blue and the Gray.

STEELDUST

QUARTER HORSE

HE looked fast, did the sturdy, short-coupled horse in the camp of strangers from up North. Texans, riding by, granted as much and they knew good stock when they saw it.

Sure thing he was fast, the owners admitted. He was tough as steel and could show his dust to anything on four legs in these parts. Fact was his name was Steeldust. He could beat any local cayuse, boasted the newcomers, and they'd be glad to prove it, if Texans were willing to put up enough cash to make it worth their while.

Neither here in the territory, which would win its independence from Mexico in a decade or so, nor anywhere else in the North American continent was there any trouble about finding that difference of opinion that makes a horse race. This one would be run over the regular straightaway distance: a quarter-mile. (Longer races over oval tracks would not come in generally until 1850.) Before the Revolution, in Virginia and the Carolinas, horses capable of running a quarter at top

speed had been developed. The type was beginning to be known, as it is today, as the quarter horse.

Perhaps Steeldust had some thoroughbred blood—not over-much, since too great an infusion meant a loss of stamina and other needed qualities in the cross. Breathe a good quarter horse a bit after a burst of speed and he would give you another and still others over rough going and he would serve you well at any sort of a task a man could fairly ask.

It was no formal race Steeldust and his Texas opponent ran that day. Riders, who never heard of racing silks, swung into the saddle and rode their mounts up to a line scratched on the ground. No drum tap, like the fancy custom up North, started them. One horseman simply passed the word to the other and they were off like a shot in the steel-spring start for which quarter horses are famed. Cowboy yells rent the sky, as the two catapulted toward the blanket, laid on the treeless prairie to mark the finish.

Yes, the people from the North had been right. Steeldust licked the local champion plenty, and no doubt about it. Pockets emptied, as the losers paid up. The grinning winners were preparing to start back home when a determined-looking delegation barred their way.

"You got our money, an' we ain't begrudgin' it," came the spokesman's Texas drawl. "But now that hoss is in this yere country, we ain't aimin' to let it leave."

Steeldust stayed in the land of his victory. He sired other racers, which were also general-utility horses, dependable under saddle or pack. From his loins sprang colts with the makings of polo ponies and many a cow-puncher's "Sunday hoss" or special "chopping hoss," handy at the tough work of a round-up. So celebrated did his get become that they and other fine quarter horses like them long were dubbed "Steeldusts."

OLD WHITEY

TARGET IN TWO WARS

AMONG the early spoils of war when General Zachary Taylor led his blue-clad army across the Rio Grande in 1846 was a snow-white charger, captured from a Mexican officer. "Old Rough and Ready," needing a new mount, approved the sturdy cob and named him Old Whitey. Climbing into the saddle, General Taylor marched onward in Mexico to win the series of victories destined to put him in the White House.

At Palo Alto and Resaca de la Palma, Taylor rode his captured charger into the thick of the fighting. No sheltered post in the rear ever suited Old Zach, veteran Regular and Indian-fighter. Whitey's color drew enemy fire like a magnet, but the General's staff, pleading with him to change to a less conspicuous mount or move out of range, met a curt refusal. Rider and horse, both steady as rock under the hail of whistling lead, stood fast.

They made no gallantly martial spectacle. Old Whitey was not given to curvetting and prancing. His master, who hated uniforms, wore a blue-checked gingham coat, blue trousers, a

Paul Brown

lemon-colored waistcoat, and a broad-brimmed straw hat and he lounged comfortably in his saddle with one leg slung over the pommel. The military Duke of Wellington, presented with a lithograph of the homespun American general on the battle-field, was so amused and impressed he directed the picture be framed and hung in the Coronation Chamber. But in action, American infantry and dragoons, streaming past to charge and break the Mexican lines, wildly cheered their commander perched, calm and cool, on his target of a white horse.

Sore feet kept Old Whitey out of the Battle of Monterey. Having "missed the fun" there, as Old Zach put it, his steed must have a part in the next fight. Taylor rode him to the top of a plateau at Buena Vista in full view of the Mexican de-fenses and well within rifle shot. Two bullets ripped through the gingham coat. An enemy battery laid on Old Whitey and opened fire. This time "Old Rough and Ready" made a slight concession to his staff's frantic protests. "I do believe the rascals want to hit me," he drawled. "We'll ride up nearer, and their balls will go over us."

After the war, at a celebration in New Orleans, Taylor dis-dained a carriage and rode his charger in the parade, and Old Whitey, regarded as a symbol of his master's victories, shared the crowd's plaudits. But he became the victim of admirers when the General dismounted for a service in the cathedral. Souvenir hunters snatched hairs from his mane and almost denuded his tail.

Zachary Taylor, elected President of the United States,

died after a few months in office. Old Whitey was retired to a life of ease on the family's southern plantation, though he still needed protection from souvenir collectors.

But in the Civil War, Union Army foragers hauled Old Whitey out of his stable. Not content with horsehairs, they were about to take the whole animal when Mrs. Richard Taylor, the General's daughter-in-law, rushed from the manor house. She begged the Yankees to take anything else but this white horse which had belonged to Zachary Taylor. However, she concealed the fact that her husband, a Confederate colonel, was even then preparing to attack the Union forces. Her pleas were futile. Sorry, said the foragers, but our colonel has to have a fresh mount. They led Old Whitey off.

So the old war horse, with the Colonel of the 14th Iowa Infantry astride, once more plunged into the fray. In the sharp engagement of Pleasant Hill (1864), the colonel was shot from his mount, mortally wounded. Captain Warren C. Jones took command of the regiment and rode Old Whitey through the rest of the battle, which ended in defeat of the Gray.

Old Whitey, sent to Iowa, was taught to plow on the dead colonel's farm. Two years later Captain Jones bought him. Well cared for during the remainder of his life, Old Whitey, veteran of two wars under four flags, was buried with military honors.

BLACK TOM

DRAGOON'S LEAPER

ON his ebony charger, a captain of the 2nd U. S. Dragoons sat awaiting orders at the Battle of Resaca de la Palma. No cavalryman was ever more splendidly mounted. Black Tom, a handsome seventeen-hand gelding, made a striking spectacle, champing his bit and pawing the Mexican plain that day in 1846. No less eye-filling was his tall rider, Charles Augustus May, his long black locks streaming from under his plumed helmet and a waist-length black beard rippling over the tunic of his smart uniform.

General Zachary Taylor turned to the dragoon. An advanced American battery, dueling with Mexican guns and threatened by hovering lancers, had asked for immediate aid.

"Charge, Captain," the general commanded.

May saluted, put himself at the head of his squadron and led a hell-for-leather charge in column of fours.

Black Tom's mane and tail streamed back in the rushing wind of a headlong gallop, vying with his master's horsehair plume and long hair and beard. Shot and shell opened gaps in the ranks, but the leader and his steed swept on unscathed.

Paul Brown

Thundering down on the Mexican battery, May launched his steed straight at a smoking cannon and cleared it with a magnificent leap, sabering a gunner as he flashed past. The charge covered a quarter of a mile before the captain could turn his troopers. Meanwhile the battery had been remanned and had to be recaptured by American infantry.

General Taylor overlooked May's losses and failure to hold the foe's guns. Not only was the dragoon brevetted lieutenant colonel but assigned to command the general's own escort, where the bearded *beau-sabreur* on his coal-black charger afforded a startling contrast to "Old Rough and Ready" in his nondescript clothes, lolling in the saddle of placid Old Whitey.

Black Tom never refused an order from his master, however foolhardy. Once during the war, May wagered he could jump a thirty-five-foot ditch. His black soared across that broad gap like a bird. He did not refuse even when the dragoon galloped him at a fifty-foot canal, but that was asking too much, and Black Tom fell short and landed his resplendent master in a bath of cold, muddy water.

Still a show-off after the war, May jumped his gelding over a loaded wood-cart in the streets of Baltimore. Undaunted by a police-court fine, he rode Black Tom up the steps of the leading hotel and through its lobby and parlors. But the horse would not put up with the whims of others. Borrowed by a man anxious to make an impression on a Baltimore belle, he tossed his rider off in front of the lady's house and galloped back to his stable.

HAMBLETONIAN

SIRE OF TROTTERS

THE new-foaled colt struggled to his feet on the stable straw and wondered at the bright world into which he had come, a world which would remember his name long after he left it. In equal wonderment, his dam gazed at him, like all mothers at their newborn offspring, and with her tongue lovingly smoothed the youngster's bay coat and the white star on his forehead, matching his white-stockinged hind legs. It did not matter that no one admired her—Kent's mare, minus pedigree and lame from hauling a butcher's cart over the cobblestones of New York. Yet she came of sturdy Conestoga stock, the horses which pulled the covered wagons of that name for settlers of the West, and the colt had the blood of the great Messenger through his sire, Abdallah.

A third present that day in 1849, Bill Rysdyck, the hired man, eyed the foal as devotedly as its mother. One of those strong attachments that sometimes spring up between a man and a horse, it grew, though passing days showed small reason for it. Even for a colt the bay was ungainly and coarse-looking. Yet the hired hand, using all his savings and credit, paid

$125 for the colt and his dam and set up to farm for himself.

The resounding name of Hambletonian was conferred on the colt. Neighbors laughed at the bay's disproportioned head, large body and legs and called him "Rysdyck's big bull."

If Hambletonian resembled a bull, it was a prize one, as appeared when his owner put him to stud. No great shakes as a trotter himself—his best time was a mile in an unimpressive 2.48—the bay stallion transmitted such speed to his get that his stud fee climbed from nothing to $25 and soared on up to $500. So many of his sons and daughters proved champions in that heyday of harness racing that Hambletonian's services were in constant demand. Before his death in 1876, he sired the astounding total of 1335 foals and raised Bill Rysdyck to affluence by his earnings of more than $186,000.

Twenty-five years after Hambletonian's passing, the automobile arrived. The harness turf declined toward the vanishing point, though running tracks continued. Surfaced highways replaced dirt roads and speedways, and stables emptied of fast-steppers. But Hambletonian's name was not destined for oblivion.

Slowly harness racing began to stage a come-back. It rose steadily until today 15,000 trotters and pacers are trained for the races on more than 500 tracks from coast to coast, and millions watch their beautiful rhythm as they flash around the course to win rich purses.

And the classic of the trotting world, run annually at Goshen, New York, is properly titled The Hambletonian.

Paul Brown

CRUISER

A TERROR AND HIS MASTER

So vicious and ferocious was the dark bay stallion, Cruiser, he would certainly have been destroyed, had he not been a valuable stud. Bred in 1852, he displayed an ugly temper even as a colt. He was raced once as a two-year-old and entered for the Derby, but fell sick. When he recovered, his disposition was more evil than ever. He kicked his stall into splinters and bit and struck at stablemen. None dared approach even to feed him; grooms sneaked fodder into the manger while Cruiser's attention was distracted and then ran. They managed to clamp a combination muzzle-bridle, reinforced with iron plates and weighing eight pounds, on the stallion's head. That restraint, worn for three years, made him wilder still.

At that time, a remarkable American, John S. Rarey of Ohio, came to England to stage exhibitions of his power over horses. As a boy he trained his pony and at twelve put on shows with horses he had taught tricks. In Texas, pitching mustangs quieted to docile mounts under his hands. Rarey did not break a horse—he used kindness, firmness, and patience, appealing to an animal's intelligence and making friends with

94

Paul Brown

him. He made no secret of his method but described it in books. It worked not only with horses but with other animals. He was able to train even stubborn zebras to harness and he schooled and drove a handsome pair of elk.

The Horse-Master's successful exhibitions in England aroused widespread attention. Inevitably they brought him a challenge. His shows were all very well, but let him try to tame Cruiser! Rarey instantly accepted.

Intent spectators, anticipating carnage, watched from a safe distance, much like crowds gathered in the Roman Colosseum to view a combat between a gladiator and a wild beast. Rarey entered the fortress-like stable of brick and oak. Twice Cruiser charged him with a stentorian bellow which no bull could have bettered. Rarey ducked out but advanced a third time and managed to tie the stallion's head to a rack. For twenty minutes Cruiser struggled madly while the strange man spoke to him and stroked him. Gradually his fury spent itself. Rarey buckled a strap to one foreleg, ran it through a loop on a surcingle and gently pulled, forcing the horse to kneel, then to lie down. He seated himself on the recumbent creature. In three hours Rarey rode him, followed by Lord Dorchester, Cruiser's owner.

Queen Victoria patted Cruiser's head with impunity. No longer did his eyes roll wildly, showing their whites, but "gleamed with a tranquil Christian brightness, warranted to carry a Bishop without risking the interests of the Church." His taming brought Rarey two thousand pupils. A waltz was composed in his honor, and such complimentary stanzas as this:

> Cruiser, who late like maniac
> Amongst the tombs long dwelt,
> Is now so meek that e'en the Queen
> His gentle head has felt.

Cruiser, hired to appear in a circus, performed excellently until the ringmaster needlessly and rashly cut him with his whip. Trumpeting his rage, the stallion reverted to savagery and chased his enemy, who barely escaped from the ring with his life. Fortunately Rarey was present. He descended from his seat into the arena, stood still and called, "Cruiser! Cruiser!" Slowly he approached and patted the trembling horse, which at once became his affectionate slave. "Kindness," declared Rarey, "is power."

Acquired and taken back to the States by Rarey, Cruiser and his master made numerous public appearances. He developed into a first-class actor, snorting and kicking rambunctiously, then submitting. Surviving his owner and friend, he died on the Rarey farm at the age of twenty-three.

GOLDSMITH MAID

GLAMOUR GIRL IN HARNESS

GRACEFUL, deer-like, the little bay mare tossed her dainty head and flashed her great, speaking eyes. She was the equine Miss America of her day, with a reign lasting not one year but thirteen. Any human actress would view her career in greenest envy. Goldsmith Maid was a star and she knew it. Her stage was the trotting track, she played to full houses from coast to coast, her publicity was terrific, and her box-office take exceeded $350,000.

None could have foretold her triumphs. While her sire was "Old Ab," Alexander's Abdallah, of Hambletonian descent, he made a poor match with a livery stable mare of no breeding. Their foal, dropped in 1857, was a harum-scarum filly, inclined to nip the unwary and so long unbreakable to harness that she was allowed to run wild until she was eight years old. Several times she changed owners for a few hundred dollars. Only after she was sold to Alden Goldsmith, whose namesake she became, did the bay mare receive good training and begin to win races.

Enter now the leading man who elevated Goldsmith Maid to stardom. He was Budd Doble, whose name sounded to Oliver

Paul Brown

Wendell Holmes like a cold in the head. Doble, one of the finest racing drivers and trainers of all time, bought the Maid for $20,000. Under his skilled hands, she stepped out with such speed that she broke the world trotting record seven times in eleven seasons, finally lowering it to a mile in two minutes and fourteen seconds. And she was hitched to a high-wheeled, sixty-pound sulky, not the light, bicycle-type vehicle of later days.

Before a race, the Maid grew so excited that her hoofs "actually chattered on the ground," but once her driver took the reins she calmed completely. Her own racing generalship worked out a plan of campaign for each heat as she trotted it, usually with no guidance whatever from the man in the sulky. If a rival drew too far ahead, she took it easy and saved herself for the next heat, knowing as well as anyone that she need only win the best three out of five. In a close finish, she never required whip or urging, but of her own accord put on the burst of speed that brought her under the wire ahead. Out of a hundred and nineteen races she won ninety-five and placed in all the rest except one. She was the greatest money-maker of the turf until 1923, when Zev, a running horse, surpassed her record.

The Maid's tours through the United States were like royal progresses. Crowds turned out just to see her go through town. They paid as high as $5000 at the gate to watch her exhibition miles against time. It was impossible to meet the public demand for a glimpse of her, though she made three trips to California, and appeared in seventeen States and on more than fifty tracks. Such was the Maid's charm that men cheered her wildly in her races and excited women snapped their fans and parasols. Articles, editorials, and a full-length biography celebrated her. Her portrait was painted in and out of harness, and her lithographs sold widely. The likeness of Goldsmith Maid hung in public buildings and homes throughout the land.

For years she never traveled without two constant companions: a mongrel dog and Old Charley, her rubber, who always slept in her stall with a feed bag under his head. The Maid, waking hungry and restless at five o'clock, would nuzzle the bag, and her groom would get up and give her an early-morning snack.

Toward the end of a career of unprecedented length—the Maid hadn't been burned out in youth—she lost a big race to a younger horse. Wisely her owner retired her from the track. Though she had reached the considerable equine age of twenty-one, she took up family life and delighted her public by becoming the mother of three foals.

Lonely and a little crochety as she grew older, Goldsmith Maid was given a crony in her pasture, a former turf rival named Lucy. The two venerable mares grazed together, apparently spending their days reminiscing happily of past glories. The Maid died at thirty in 1885 and was buried beneath a monument, proclaiming the sum of her winnings. Yet it was not money that made the mare go. The Maid raced for the love of it and the cheers of the crowds for her, their favorite.

TWO-BITS

VETERAN OF INDIAN WARS

"**W**OULD the liftinint like to buy a fine horse?" came the query.

At rigid but anxious attention, Joe Cain, Irish-born fifer of a U. S. Infantry company, faced the officer he was questioning.

Lieutenant Charles A. Curtis, acting quartermaster of the frontier fort at Prescott, Arizona, refused. Already mounted, he could not afford a second horse. But this, the soldier persisted, was a bargain. As one of sixteen horses ridden into the ground by a volunteer cavalry outfit in a seven-hundred-mile march and condemned to be sold at public auction, he could be bought for five dollars, halter included. Lieutenant Curtis was highly skeptical that any such miserable wreck could be of use to him, but handed over the money out of fondness for the soldier, who had served him faithfully as his striker, or personal orderly.

Some days later Cain reported with the animal, a large bay with a white star on his forehead, restored to splendid condition by good care. Astounded, the officer heard the horse's story.

Paul Brown

Cain had come upon a man beating and kicking a prone nag to make him rise, while the poor creature struggled weakly and vainly. The Irishman, stepping in front of the human brute, recognized his victim from their service together in the Mounted Rifles in 1858, and the horse knew him, since he lifted his head to thrust his muzzle appealingly into his old friend's hand. This bay was the troop horse Cain had ridden in a race in which his chances were generally supposed not to be worth two-bits—twenty-five cents. He had galloped to victory by three lengths, winning both the prize and a name for his mount: Two-Bits. Now the orderly proudly turned him over to the officer who had bought him.

On two occasions Two-Bits saved his new owner's life. Once, grazing unpicketed while Curtis fished, the horse trotted back in excitement. The officer hastily swung into the saddle and sighted a party of mounted Apaches, about to ride down on him. Two-Bits' long strides outdistanced pursuit. Again, Lieutenant Curtis was riding unsuspectingly along a road, with his left foot out of the stirrup, when a bullet ripped through his coat collar and unhorsed him. Two-Bits never stirred until he was remounted, then swiftly carried his rider away from the Apache ambush.

All the garrison had come to know Two-Bits as a comrade when the horse was sent on his last detail.

An important dispatch had to be forwarded to Santa Fe through Indian country so dangerous that no express rider could be hired. The route was strewn with the stripped, scalped, mutilated bodies of too many who had risked it. Sometimes parties of ten or fifteen cavalrymen were massacred in the attempt. In the present emergency, a brave and able sergeant named Porter volunteered, providing he could ride Two-Bits. Private mount though the horse was, Lieutenant Curtis consented.

Four days Sergeant Porter and Two-Bits traveled steadily, snatching rest when they could. Nearing rocky, hilly country, the bay of his own accord took a side-track and short of a crest halted in sudden alarm. Porter spotted four Indian ponies behind boulders. Unquestionably their owners were lying in wait along the regular road. Aware he had escaped certain death and now could skirt the ambush with a fair chance of winning clear, the sergeant patted his horse's face and spoke affectionately to him: "Now, old fellow, everything depends on your legs."

Porter killed one of the Indian ponies with his carbine and galloped for his life. Three Navajos vaulted on the others' backs and clattered after him, yipping shrill war whoops. Steadily they gained—Two-Bits was old and for days had lacked his accustomed feed of grain. The sergeant, turning in his saddle, picked off one pursuer with a marvelous shot, but the survivors came on, firing. A bullet smashed into his right hand, and his carbine fell from his grasp. Twice more he was hit in the back. Two-Bits shuddered in his course—Indian lead was finding its mark in him also—but his long stride never faltered.

A lucky revolver shot stopped a second Navajo. Porter paid for it when the remaining Indian sent a bullet thudding into his ribs. Desperately, the cavalryman wheeled and, riding straight down on his startled assailant, fired his last round into the Indian mustang's brain.

Two-Bits and his rider, both badly wounded, struggled on. As night fell, a blaze winked in the distance. Porter could not make it. He fainted and reeled from his saddle to the ground. Two-Bits, bleeding from six wounds, dragged himself on to the wagon-train, camped by the fire, where his appearance sent men out to find and save the sergeant. His duty done, the charger staggered, fell and died.

Over the grave where they buried him they heaped stones and fired the three volleys which are a soldier's right. Years saw the stones rise to a pyramid, for every passing trooper added one in tribute to a gallant veteran.

WINCHESTER (RIENZI)

"AND SHERIDAN TWENTY MILES AWAY"

COAL-BLACK except for white stockings on all but his off hind leg, the three-year-old gelding inherited his beauty, intelligence, and endurance from his ancestor, Black Hawk, a noted Morgan. The black was one of the handsomest horses in the Union Army. His owner, an officer of the 2nd Michigan Cavalry, regarded him with pride and admiration but never rode him. Before the Civil War, that officer never had been on a horse. The black gelding, young and fiery, stood more than seventeen hands high, and his back seemed a long way from the ground. Preferring a quieter mount, the black's master invited the regimental commander to try his spirited steed.

The stocky colonel climbed up into the saddle, wrapped his cavalryman's bow-legs around the Morgan's barrel and sat the prancing animal like a centaur. It was one of those perfect matches between man and horse. These two would ride into history together, for the colonel was Phil Sheridan, who would become a lieutenant-general and the foremost Union cavalry leader.

Officers of the regiment, seeing how taken their colonel was with the horse, clubbed together, bought him from his owner and presented him. Sheridan named him Rienzi after the Mississippi town where the regiment was encamped that spring of 1863, and rode him constantly through the rest of the war in the many actions, raids, and full-scale campaigns in which he took part. The Morgan, an extraordinarily fast walker, covered five miles an hour at that gait to the dismay of the general's staff, whose mounts had to break into a dog-trot to keep up. The black seemed to thrive on long marches and short rations, and was never ill. In a war where horse casualties were so high that the Union Army required five hundred remounts a day, Rienzi escaped with four wounds, none of which kept him long off duty.

It was in the Shenandoah Valley that the black won fame and a new name. Sheridan was absent from the field, making a report in Washington, when the Confederates struck his troops at Cedar Creek. The Gray tide swept over the Blue defenses and rolled them back in a retreat that was fast becoming a disorderly rout when General Sheridan returned and heard the news at Winchester. Swinging into his charger's saddle, Sheridan galloped toward the battlefront nearly twenty miles away. As he met his blue-clad troops streaming back, the General reined in. "We're all right. Never mind, boys, we'll whip 'em yet." Flourishing his hat, he waved them forward. Men rallied, cheered Sheridan and his foam-flecked steed, turned and surged after him into the fight. The Gray ranks, slow in

following up their advantage, were smashed back, their victory transformed into defeat.

The General and his mount, called Winchester from that day, were immortalized in Thomas Buchanan Read's poem, "Sheridan's Ride."

> Be it said in letters both bold and bright:
> "Here is the steed that saved the day
> By carrying Sheridan into the fight,
> From Winchester twenty miles away."

During the last eight years of Winchester's life, Sheridan saw to it that he was never worked, only given necessary exercise. "He has become a little rheumatic, fat and lazy," the General wrote, "but he has fairly earned his rest, and as long as I live he will be taken care of."

Winchester, dying in 1878, was skillfully mounted by a taxidermist and placed as a relic in the military museum on Governor's Island, New York. For years afterwards, veterans of Sheridan's Shenandoah command crossed to the island every Memorial Day to lay wreaths beside the glass case containing the remains of the black charger.

TRAVELLER

LEE'S BELOVED GRAY

THE handsome gray, black-maned head held high, flaunting his black tail, won Robert E. Lee's heart at first sight that day in 1861 during a campaign in the Virginia mountains. The General commanding the Armies of the Confederacy asked the young soldier riding the four-year-old if he would sell him. Willingly, came the answer, but the horse was already promised to a captain. Lee, no man to take advantage of his rank, nodded. Yet whenever he saw the gray, he longed for him, speaking affectionately of him as "my colt." He could not forego repeating his offer to the captain, who at once tried to present the horse to the beloved leader of the victorious troops of the South. Refusing to accept a gift, General Lee paid $200 and renamed his mount, originally dubbed Jeff Davis or Greenbrier, calling him Traveller because of his swift, untiring gaits.

So began a devoted companionship between man and horse, to endure through the stirring and tragic events of the Civil War and beyond. Lee's string included several other mounts, but Traveller always stood first. The "Confederate gray," over

sixteen hands, a little above half-bred, would prick up his deli-
cate ears and come to his master's whistle. No horse was ever
more fortunate in his owner. A fine horseman, Lee had commanded U. S. cavalry regiments before he gave his loyalty to
his native state of Virginia, seceding from the Union, and his
love and care for horses extended beyond his own to all animals
in the Confederate armies. Frequently he inspected shoeing,
girthing, throat latches, and the folding of saddle blankets.
In the field he dismounted as often as possible to rest his mount
and demanded that others show the same consideration.

Through most of the great battles, Lee rode Traveller,
curvetting, nostrils flaring, hoofs pounding an echo to the roll-
ing volleys and the thundering cannonade. Glimpses of the
gray General on his gray charger lived in the memories of
men who saw them in action. Only once did Traveller partly
fail his master. At the Second Manassas (Bull Run), Lee was
standing beside him when a shout of "Yankee cavalry!" made
the horse jump. Lee reached for the bridle, tripped and fell,
injuring both hands so that he could not hold reins and was
compelled to ride in an ambulance for some days. In desperate
moments both in the Wilderness and at Spotsylvania, officers
and men barely prevented the General from spurring Traveller
forward to lead a charge on the advancing bluecoats. Artillery
fire at the latter battle caused the gray to rear, and in that
instant a shell passed under his girth, missing his rider's stirrup
by inches.

And none who witnessed it would forget a vivid scene in

the final rally before the South went down in defeat, when General Lee, erect in his saddle, held aloft a battle flag, and Traveller tossed his head proudly in answer to the salutes of ragged regiments swinging past into their last vain fight.

Closer than ever in peace was the comradeship cemented in battle. During the years "Marse Robert" served as president of Washington and Lee University in Virginia, he took daily rides on Traveller and spoke of their "perfect understanding." Sometimes children, thrilled to the core, were permitted to mount the famous war horse.

Traveller survived his master and was led in his funeral, marching with other old comrades-in-arms. A few years later the gray died of lockjaw, deeply grieved by the Lee family.

Lee and Traveller live in the pages of history, on canvases, sculptured in bronze, immortal and inseparable as always.

BLACK KETTLE

QUARRY OF HORSE HUNTERS

$\mathbf{A}$LL the broad plains spread before the black yearling, and his nostrils drank in the scent of freedom, strange but glorious. Wariness quickly had replaced the terror of that dawn in 1867 when Cheyennes swooped down on a Mormon wagon train and ran him off along with other Kentucky thoroughbreds, westward-bound with the emigrants. The stud colt had kicked up his heels and escaped the Indians. To them he owed his liberty, and men came to call him Black Kettle after the chief of the band.

Growth and strength gained, he did battle with other stallions of the wild horse herds. Soon he was lord over more than a score of mares, and fine colts that he had sired frisked in his train. Many men saw and coveted the magnificent black, galloping away, marshaling and guarding his family, his luxuriant mane and long tail streaming. Finest horse in the West, they called him.

For years, Indians, plainsmen and settlers tried to capture him. Once a cavalry captain took out his whole troop in an attempt to round up Black Kettle. He broke through their cordon. None succeeded in running him down or "creasing" him—stunning a mustang by severing a nerve at the top of his neck with a bullet. Black Kettle, swift and crafty, evaded them all. Only the fact that he was often seen kept him from becoming a legend, like ghost horses of the plains, vainly pursued by red men and white for decades.

In 1879 an expert wild horse hunter, Frank M. Lockard, and his partner took Black Kettle's trail. Like all the rest, they failed and rode home after they were caught in a night blizzard that froze the partner's feet.

Next year Lockard, young and determined, made another try. "I knew," he said, "if I followed that horse long and far enough, he would give up." Driving a pair in an open buggy, the hunter slowly and steadily trailed Black Kettle day·after day, camping nights. Lockard gave his quarry little rest. Back and forth they criss-crossed the prairie. Seven times the hunter changed teams and nearly killed one in a hot thirty-mile gallop after the stampeding stallion and his twenty-seven mares and their foals.

Black Kettle shook off his pursuer, only to be picked up again. Lockard knew the water holes where the fugitives must drink. Some of the mares were limping now, and colts began dropping back. Black Kettle, in the post of danger at the rear, strove to gather them in and hurry them on.

On the thirtieth day of that epic chase, luck turned against the weary Black Kettle. With Lockard close behind, he led his bunch toward a ranch house in strange country. The wild

horses blundered into a corral. Lockard, proud and happy, closed the gate behind them.

Next day his captor roped Black Kettle. The stallion lunged at the fence, got one foot over, was dragged back. His freedom was ended. Broken to saddle, then to harness, he was matched and teamed with another fine animal named Black Pot. Lockard, the thrill of the chase over, sold him. Several times more he changed hands. He lived to the age of thirty-nine, hauling freight and milk wagons, pulling a plow.

Rather let him be remembered from the days when he roamed the prairie, wild and free, a challenge and a quest.

MAIDAN

CAMPAIGNER AND STEEPLECHASER

THE path of the chestnut Arabian, foaled in Nejd in 1868, led, as for many others of his kind, to the rich horse markets of India. An agent for some fabulously wealthy rajah might have bought him. However, it happened that on the day of sale the purse of a British officer was large enough to bid him in. Maidan's purchaser was a lucky man.

The Briton entered him, though only a two-year-old, in a classic event—the Punjab cup. Maidan raced through the field like a pestilence—the meaning of his name in Hindustani—blighted the high hopes of the Australian favorite and emptied the pockets of his backers. By 1874 the chestnut had won so many races that no further matches could be made, and his owner sold him.

Maidan now became the charger of a Scottish officer, who with his equipment weighed two hundred and sixty-six pounds. The Arabian was a small horse like most of his breed, standing under fifteen hands, but possessed their astonishing strength and stamina in full measure. He carried his heavy rider through twelve years of hard mountain campaigning in India and Afghanistan. He was of the valiant company of those war horses which the Koran, like the Bible, sings in glowing poetry— "snorting steeds whose hoofs dash sparks of fire as they scour to the attack at dawn and stir the dust aloft, cleaving through the midst of a host."

When the Scot was killed in one of Lord Roberts' battles, Maidan returned to peaceful pursuits. He won the Ganges Hog Hunt Cup, a four-mile steeplechase over difficult country, and a series of other steeplechases and flat races.

Becoming the property of another British officer, he was embarked for England on a troopship, which at Suez was diverted to duty as a transport for an expedition. Not for one hundred days did Maidan set foot on land and, during that period, stable guards below decks testified that he never once lay down. Yet he continued so fit he won three steeplechases in England at the age of twenty and another the next year.

At twenty-three, the amazing Arab, still absolutely sound, broke a leg in the hunting field and had to be destroyed.

Paul Brown

COMANCHE

SURVIVOR OF CUSTER'S LAST STAND

FAR better than recruits, as well as
any old-time trooper in Custer's 7th Cavalry, the horse Comanche recognized and obeyed the trumpet calls. At drill, he
proudly took his rightful place at the head of Company "I,"
with never a touch on his reins. His rider was the company
commander, Captain Myles W. Keogh, hard-fighting soldier
of fortune, who had served with the Papal Zouaves, in North
African campaigns, through our own Civil War, and now in
conflict with the Indians.

Comanche was a bay gelding, standing only fifteen hands,
and no registered thoroughbred. Yet in his veins ran the blood
of steeds the Conquistadores brought from Spain, and through
them descent could be claimed for him from the chariot horses
of the Pharoahs and the Arabs and Barbs of the Saracens. His
was the strength, intelligence, and stamina of an ideal cavalry
mount. Keogh had purchased him from the Government remount service at his cost price of $90.

Comanche curvetted under Keogh on a May day in 1876
when the mounted band played the Seventh's battle song,

Paul Brown

Garryowen, and Custer led his regiment out of Fort Abraham Lincoln to fight the Sioux and Cheyennes. Untiringly, the little bay carried his master on the long march toward the fatal valley of the Little Big Horn.

History relates how the Indians' fine war chief, Crazy Horse, dealt with the three Army columns attempting to converge on him—defeating and flinging back General Crook and waiting to give Custer battle in the valley before the third force could come up. When Custer discovered the vast Indian camp at the Little Big Horn, he split up his regiment into three battalions and confidently ordered attack. Even with the Seventh undivided, the odds would have been far too great: six hundred cavalrymen against two thousand five hundred red warriors.

Yelping hordes shattered Reno's battalion in a bloody repulse, then swept back to meet Custer's charge on the other end of the village.

Comanche's hoofs drummed on the plain, as Keogh and his company, riding with Custer's contingent, galloped into action. A furious Indian onrush hurled them back, surrounded them. Under a hail of bullets and arrows, the blue ranks melted away. War clubs crashed on troopers' skulls, and scalping knives flashed in the sun. It was all over in one brief, desperate hour. Yellow-haired Custer lay dead on the knoll where he made his last stand, and strewn about him were the bodies of over two hundred cavalrymen who had followed him into battle.

The other two battalions, besieged on a hill, barely held

out until the third Army column rescued them. The sight of stripped, white bodies led them to the scene of Custer's disaster. Vainly they scanned the plain for any living creature.

From a ravine sounded a plaintive whinny. Limping painfully, saddle dangling under his belly, appeared a gravely wounded cavalry horse. It was Comanche, the only survivor on the battlefield.

Surgeons tended his wounds. Slowly and gently, he was led fifteen miles to a waiting supply ship on the Yellowstone River and transported back to the post. There, for a year, a sling supported him in his stall until he was healed. By regimental order he never was ridden again. Saddled and bridled, the honored veteran was led by a trooper in all the Seventh's parades. Sometimes he broke loose and trotted to the head of his old company. He could graze on gardens with impunity, and on pay days soldiers treated him to buckets of beer. Comanche lived to a ripe old age, dying in 1891.

SLEEPY TOM

HE RACED THROUGH DARKNESS

O FTEN, the fate of horses is to change owners. It may be the heartless discard of a nag, grown old in service, or a reluctant parting with a favorite whose keep can no longer be afforded. A breeder's auction, or a selling-platter race, man's fondness for a horse-swap, or a score of other reasons. Whatever the motive, a succession of masters is far more common for the horse than for those other close companions of mankind, the dog and the cat.

To change hands frequently and usually for the worse was Sleepy Tom's lot during the first twelve years of his life.

Sleepy Tom was a pacer, both legs on the same side moving forward and backward together—opposite to a trotter's leg action. Because of that lateral motion, pacers were mockingly called "side-wheelers," though many a joker forgot the crack when he watched the speed of pacers on the harness tracks. But in spite of great sires in his blood line—American Eclipse and Messenger—Sleepy Tom never woke up and won races. Repeatedly he was sold. Once he was traded for a three-year-

Paul Brown

old colt, a cheap watch, and a quart of whisky—total value, thirty dollars.

One day in 1878, a noted racing driver, Stephen C. Phillips, encountered a broken-down plug with a familiar look. Recognition was not easy, although he himself had owned the horse some years before. Since then neglect and ill treatment had taken a heavy toll. But the animal was undeniably Sleepy Tom and now, more than ever, he lived up to his name. His eyes were as blank and unseeing as a sleep-walker's. He had become stone-blind.

It was not remorse that made Phillips buy Sleepy Tom back; the driver, when he had sold him, could not know that the horse would suffer cruel usage. Pity must have played a part, but there was something more. Phillips had a hunch. He gave Sleepy Tom the best of care and on his recovery put him back into training.

Ohio tracks that year saw a new entry—a blind, twelve-year-old pacer. Sleepy Tom, one of his biographers declares, "was the laughing-stock of the crowds before his races, a hero after them." Spectators watched the old side-wheeler speed out in front. Sightless eyes staring, he trusted perfectly in the guidance of the reins in Phillips' sure hands. All through every heat he cocked his ears for his driver's voice. It came to him steadily over the thud of flying hoofs, giving him confidence, encouragement, and orders he instantly obeyed. He won race after race. That season Sleepy Tom lowered the world record to 2:22½ minutes.

In one race Sleepy Tom was crowded against the rail, spokes ripped from a wheel of his rig, and Phillips pitched from his seat. The blind pacer halted. Though another horse caromed against him, almost knocking him down, he stood fast until his driver climbed back in behind him, gathered in the lines and drove on.

The hunch paid off again in '79. Sleepy Tom made the Grand Circuit, winning over star pacers, old and new. In Michigan he paced the six fastest heats thus far raced in harness. In Chicago, at the age of thirteen, he once more broke the world's pacing record with a heat of 2:12¼, nosing out the great Mattie Hunter in a race so close that watches could not clock the difference in time.

Records fall. Sleepy Tom's stood until 1881 when another pacer bettered it. But the memory of the gallant blind horse flashing around a track through the darkness enveloping him —that will always stand.

DANDY

CAVALRY AND BUFFALOES

WHEN the 7th U. S. Cavalry was stationed in Kansas and Indian Territory during the winter of 1868–69, a draft of five hundred remounts was sent the regiment. The commanding officer, Lt. Col., Brevet Maj. Gen., George Armstrong Custer, sat in front of his tent and watched the new arrivals led past—bays, blacks, sorrels, grays—to be assigned to the companies riding horses matching their color.

Custer's keen horseman's eyes singled out a small, spirited bay gelding with a swagger to his gait. Already Old Curley, as his troopers called him, owned a string of chargers, including the Kentucky thoroughbred, Vic. But he needed another mount; no cavalryman rode harder on an Indian chase or a hunt. Exercising his privilege, he picked the trim bay, paid his cost of $140 to the Government and named him Dandy.

With the lively Dandy it was always up and away and find your stirrups while reining in. Seldom was he seen to walk—he stepped out with a dancing trot. On tough winter campaigns against the Indians, other horses drooped when

Paul Brown

food ran out, but Dandy scraped through snow to find grass and forged ahead as sturdily as ever.

He loved to frolic with Custer's pack of forty dogs, staghounds, greyhounds, and foxhounds, and was always careful never to step on any in the playful scuffles. Nor was he less eager than they when his master swung into his saddle, sounded a hunting horn and coursed deer, buffalo, wolves, coyotes, or jack-rabbits. Dandy became the best buffalo horse in the regiment. The minute his buckskin-clad rider chose his quarry from the thundering herd, Dandy closed in at the gallop. If a shaggy, horned head menaced him, the bay leaped aside at a sharp tangent. Then, without any guidance, he cut in again to bring Custer into position for a rifle shot at the vulnerable spot behind the bison's shoulder. Once he was not quite agile enough. A big bull suddenly wheeled, gored Dandy in the side and heaved him into the air. But the handy little horse lit on his feet, sprang away and saved himself and his master.

Dandy and Vic were Custer's mounts on the long march to the fatal Battle of the Little Big Horn in 1876. It happened that the former had been ridden more often en route, so the General left him at the wagon-train, and it was the thoroughbred, Vic, he rode into combat. When red masses of Sioux and Cheyennes overwhelmed Custer and the battalion of the Seventh he led, no living creature remained on that stricken field but the badly wounded mount of Captain Myles Keogh, Comanche.

Dandy, spared by chance, was given by the widowed Mrs.

Custer to the General's father, who had lost three sons in the battle. For the rest of his life the bay faithfully and quietly carried the old gentleman on frequent rides. Only on patriotic occasions when bands played and men paraded, did Dandy revert from his staid ways. Then he tossed his head and pranced along, legs twinkling in the old dancing trot, as he lived once more the days when he was the charger of a dashing, yellow-haired cavalryman.

MARESA

VICTORY FOR AUSTRIA

THE long-distance race, set for the fall of 1892 between the most dashing cavalrymen of Prussia and Austria, was certain to be a hard-riding, hell-for-leather affair, with no contestant sparing himself or failing to exact the last ounce of speed and endurance from his mount. Strong national rivalries guaranteed as much, and the day of cavalry and all its proud tradition had not yet altogether faded.

Stretching over the four hundred and twenty-five miles between the cities of Vienna and Berlin—the Austrians starting from their capital and the Prussians from theirs—the course was enough to tax any rider, any horse to cover in winning time. A competitor could count on little rest; he would have to ride at a rate considerably better than a hundred miles in twenty-four hours to be in the running and hold that grueling pace for at least three days and nights.

Hussars and Uhlans, all the division of the cavalry arm, scoured their stables and the stud farms of their country for mounts best able to carry their colors to triumph. One of the least impressive in appearance was the choice of Lieutenant

Paul Brown

Miklos of Austria: a small Magyar horse, a bay gelding named Maresa.

No parade horse Maresa, and light for the shock of a cavalry charge, but he was well fitted for the terrific task before him. In his ancestry was Arab blood, crossed with the tough breed of the Austrian mountains. His dam was one of the agile mounts used to ride herd on horses pastured in the valleys between the heights. Those who knew her story understood why Lieutenant Miklos had picked her colt for the endurance race.

One night a burglary had occurred fifty miles from the herd's stud farm. A herder, accused, was acquitted when he proved an alibi by witnesses who had seen him at eight o'clock in the evening and at four in the morning of the date of the crime. Not until the man fell ill and believed he was dying did he confess his guilt. He had ridden Maresa's dam fifty miles over the mountains, committed the burglary, then galloped fifty back in an amazing total of seven hours.

Twenty million marks had been wagered on the outcome of the great race when the two groups of horsemen started from Vienna and Berlin. Out of one hundred and seventeen entries only seventy-one would finish. Forty-six Prussians and Austrians, determined to win for their country, rode at so reckless and merciless a pace that their mounts died under them. Prince Leopold of Prussia, stimulating his horse with morphine injections, was the first to reach Vienna, but bad news awaited him there. A competitor had arrived earlier in Berlin.

Maresa's drumming hoofs left mile after mile behind. One hundred miles from Berlin, an unseasonably early and heavy snowstorm fell. Plunging through its drifts, the Magyar steed stumbled with weariness, but Miklos sustained him with drafts of brandy, and he forged ahead. With only thirteen hours' rest throughout the ride, the little horse and his rider, both close to exhaustion, crossed the finish line first at Tempelhof Field, three days, one hour, and forty-five minutes from the moment they left Vienna—far better time than that of the leading Prussian. Victory for Austria!

DAN PATCH

SALESMAN ON THE HOOF

"SOLD!" shouted the auctioneer at the horse sale. He grinned broadly as he banged his gavel, pointing it toward a friend in the front row.

The friend looked up, startled. A rangy, mahogany bay, with crooked hind legs and big hocks, had been knocked down to him—and he hadn't even bid. All right, he'd be a sport about it. The nag had cost him only a couple of hundred dollars.

But the joke wasn't on him after all. His purchase, Dan Patch, foaled in 1896, had Hambletonian blood. Queer legs notwithstanding, he won his maiden race in the creditable time of 2:16. He piled up victories, picking up speed until he paced a mile in 1:55¼, the fastest time thus far made under harness. Though the record was not allowed, since it was made behind a pacemaker, it was not surpassed until 1938 and then only by a quarter-second.

The next time the bay stallion was sold, he brought $60,000, top price of the day for a pacer.

That sum was more than the price of good horseflesh; it was an advertising appropriation. Dan's buyer, M. E. Savage

Paul Brown

of Minneapolis, manufactured stock feed. Dan Patch was put
right on the sales staff.

No spectator at Dan's races and numerous exhibitions was
allowed to forget his owner's product. Savage dramatized the
exhibitions by using one running horse as a pacemaker and
another as the field. Dan pounded around the track in marvelous rhythm, never breaking, and matching gallops with his
pacing. Crowds averaging 60,000 thronged to his performances
in 1904, when he made a 10,000-mile tour in his private railroad car. On his return to his home town, he was met by a band
and a parade of two thousand cheering fans. In 1905, 80,000
swamped a course to watch him. It has been estimated that in
seven years his "gates" grossed a million dollars, with another
million credited to him as a super-salesman.

Dan was intelligent, gentle and friendly. He liked people,
and people liked Dan. Newspapers spoke of him as "an ami-
able and social horse." He had an endearing trick of turning
his head from side to side and nodding, as if to greet folks
assembled in his honor. Advance agents heralded Dan's appearances at tracks with placards reading: "If you've been
there before, he'll recognize you and bow."

Dan enjoyed being photographed, and no camera could
catch him unposed. His farrier sold as souvenirs thousands of
"genuine Dan Patch horseshoes." Cigars, children's sleds, and
hobby horses were named after him. So was a washing-machine,
guaranteed to go almost as fast as Dan Patch. His portrait
was painted, widely reproduced and displayed in as many

gathering places as "Custer's Last Stand." His public eagerly read accounts of his exploits and home life and sent stamps for an illustrated booklet about him. Yet this valuable horse was by no means pampered. Winters, Savage's son, would hitch him to a sleigh and drive Dan through the snowy streets of Minneapolis.

After his racing career was over, he was retired to stud and quartered in a luxurious steam-heated, electrically-lit stable, with fourteen hundred windows and an indoor track. Many admirers traveled over a special line called "The Dan Patch Railroad" to his farm to visit and pay him homage.

RODNEY

FIELD ARTILLERY WHEELER

RODNEY, a big, handsome bay with black points, joined the U. S. Army in 1896. His size and pulling power, heritage of his Clydesdale strain, marked him as an ideal wheel horse for the field artillery. Soon Rodney knew where he belonged. Harnessed, he took his place by the limber pole and was hitched in beside his teammate. In front of them, the traces of swing and lead pairs were hooked in. "Mount!" blared a trumpet, and drivers swung up into the saddles of near horses, cannoneers to limber, gun, and caisson seats. "Forward, ho!" and Rodney was first to put his weight against his collar, as the battery rolled on.

Willing he was always. He worked so hard he sometimes broke his harness, and he was never sick. In the several regiments in which he served, Rodney won the artillerymen's affections.

War with Spain, and Rodney was shipped to Cuba with Grimes' Battery of the 2nd Artillery. Through the humid heat, they moved up to the front at El Poso. Carriages mired and stuck in the deep, clinging mud. Rodney and his teammate,

Paul Brown

Shaw, unhitched from their limber, were hooked in to help other teams and hauled them free until all Grimes' guns could go into action. At Santiago, that strong wheel pair were sent to the aid of another battery's bogged-down caisson, and the two alone pulled it out.

Home again, Rodney, with his battery, made a seven-hundred-mile march, averaging twenty-one miles a day, and outlasted all his fellows. He was transferred to the 3rd Field Artillery. In that regiment's stirring mounted drills in the Fort Myer, Virginia, riding hall, spectators admiringly watched the lively, intelligent bay wheeler, thundering around the ring with his team at a full gallop.

Not until he was twenty-eight did the years tell on Rodney. Given light duty, he was left at the stables one day while his outfit, "D" Battery, went on a hike. What then befell is best told by a heart-warming military letter, written by the battery commander, Capt. Charles G. Mortimer, to the Adjutant General:

1. In August, 1916, while the Battery was out in the field, there was left behind an old horse, name, "Rodney," who had faithfully done his work in the organization for many years, and who through age and other infirmities was unable to further pull his bit. Through ignorance of a man left behind in charge of quarters he showed the horse to an Inspector, who came to the post, and as a result he was inspected, condemned and ordered sold. The men of the battery heard of the matter just in time to have a representative at the sale and bid the horse in, as they could not bear to see the old fellow sold outside the service. He brought something like $120, which was subscribed and paid for by the men of the organization.

2. Since that time this horse has remained a pet and an inspiration to the men of the battery and a favorite among the officers, and has been fed, groomed and cared for by the battery. . . .

3. This horse is an inspiration and though unable to accompany the battery in the field, should be cared for at the post, as has been done in the case of other "retired" animals (old "Putnam" and old "Foxhall," both of the 3rd Field Artillery).

4. It is requested that the authority be granted to stable, forage and care for this animal wherever he may be for the balance of his life.

It took nineteen indorsements but, to the honor of the service, the order requested was issued. The men of Battery "D," still grinning with triumph over the mean-spirited dealer, who had tried to bid Rodney away from them at the auction, cherished their beloved wheel horse the remainder of his life. In his retirement, Rodney, for needed exercise, was used to hoist hay bales to a loft. The old fellow soon caught on and whenever he saw a load of hay arriving, galloped away from the stables.

A fine short story was written about him and made into a motion picture. Nowadays the guns he pulled are self-propelled or truck-drawn, but Rodney will always live in every field artilleryman's heart.

MANIFESTO

SUPER-STEEPLECHASER

MANIFESTO well knew the formidable obstacles he would face that March day in 1897 at the classic Grand National, England's famed steeplechase. He had met them before. The water jumps he must clear: Beecher's Brook, named for the rider spilled into it at the first Grand National in 1839, and Valentine's. The fences and thorn hedges, none over five feet—not too high to bother a good jumper— but in front of them "yawners," ditches six feet wide and three deep. Sharp swerves to the left to be made, such as Canal Turn. Not simply smooth turf but ploughed ground. Nothing was missing in the four-mile steeplechase course at Aintree, near Liverpool, except the steeple which originally gave these races their name when they were ridden cross-country, and jockeys fixed their eyes on the spire of a church as a guide toward the finish.

Twice before Manifesto had encountered those thirty redoubtable jumps, downfall of many a horse and rider. The trim bay, by Man of War (English) out of Vae Victis, had finished a creditable fourth in his first race in 1895. But next

146

Paul Brown

year he had fallen unluckily and ignominiously at the very first jump. Small wonder he was no favorite today.

Twenty-eight steeplechasers paraded before England's royalty, peers of the realm, and thronging commoners. Manifesto handily cleared the single hurdle, at that time required of each horse before the start. Then the crowd roared as the lifting barrier released a torrent of bright silks and glistening hides.

One horse after another crashed in the mighty leaps or was pulled up, unable to finish the grueling race. Seeming a true son of the winged horse, Pegasus, Manifesto soared over fence and water, thundered into the lead of the field of ten stayers and won by twenty lengths.

The following year he was entered again but had to be scratched. A careless groom had left the door of his box-stall open, and the bay had run out, leaped a five-foot gate and rapped a fetlock. But in 1899, carrying heavy weight, Manifesto won the Grand National again as the favorite, though at one fence he over-jumped so far he almost stood on his head, yet made a marvelous recovery. He placed third in 1900, 1902, and 1903. Aintree gave him one of its most rousing ovations when in 1904 the gallant old horse, then sixteen and burdened with a hundred and sixty-nine pounds, finished seventh. He is still acclaimed Grand National's greatest.

Manifesto's end was one of fate's most ironic tricks. The veteran steeplechaser, which had fallen only once in his entire racing career, stumbled while ambling around his paddock, broke a leg and had to be destroyed.

HANS

LOVE OF LEARNING AND VICE VERSA

CLEVER HANS, they called the stallion of the Russian Orloff strain, and his title was well deserved. In 1900 an eccentric, elderly German, Wilhelm von Osten, bought him and began to educate him. Painstakingly he taught Hans to distinguish right from left, top from bottom. Next the pupil learned to strike as many blows with a forefoot as he saw objects on a table; then to recognize figures written on a blackboard and thud a hoof four times for a "4" and so on.

Von Osten devised an alphabet, with "A" represented by one hoofbeat, "B" by two, and carried on thus to the middle. To save too frequent beats, the sequence was reversed at the end of the alphabet where Hans struck once for a "Z." If there were doubt about which letter the horse meant when he was spelling out a word, he was asked, "Forward or backward?" and he indicated the former by one stroke, the latter by two. Clever Hans answered questions, spelling phonetically. He did sums, told the time and the date and knew a chord from a discord. His intelligence equaled that of a schoolboy of fourteen, his master claimed.

Hans's fame spread abroad. A committee of professors, veterinarians, and cavalrymen witnessed his marvelous feats. Though they offered no explanation of them, they reported they suspected no trickery on Von Osten's part. But the next investigators snorted that Hans was only obeying secret signs from his master. The old trainer died embittered.

Hans was taken over by Herr Krall of Elberfeld, a well-to-do jeweler. Under his tutelage, based on kindness and sympathy, whereas with Von Osten it often had been a clash of wills, Hans's education advanced. He was surpassed by another of Krall's equine scholars, Muhamed, said to be capable of complicated calculations in square and cube roots. Krall asked no fees for the exhibitions. A skeptical American reporter was convinced when the horses performed for him, with Krall out of the room.

Was it telepathy—some sort of psychic control—or hypnotism? Scientific commissions supplied a variety of answers. There remained many doubters who admitted that the performances of the Elberfeld horses was remarkable but could only be ascribed to some trick. Krall himself insisted that he had only taught the horses—one of his pupils was blind—to use their own mental powers.

For years Hans had been content with praise and rewards of carrots for his achievements. Then one day a groom carelessly placed a mare in the yard adjoining Hans's enclosure.

Paul Brown

Like other cloistered scholars before and since, the stallion discovered in himself a stronger emotion than the love of learning. In his efforts to reach the mare, he cut his head and belly so severely he had to be retired.

HEATHERBLOOM

CHAMPION TIMBER-TOPPER

THUNDER *and lightning, Alarums and excursions. Enter* **HEATHERBLOOM.**

Thus might have read stage directions for the bay jumper's ring entrances, with off-stage noises of banging hoofs and shouting grooms. He burst out of the corridor in a flurry of tanbark. While his rider sat tight, Heatherbloom delighted the crowds by a bucking exhibition no rodeo mustang could better. Then he whirled, headed for the first jump and got down to business.

Foaled in 1896, Heatherbloom was bought as a green colt in Canada by Howard Willetts for the high price of $1000. Taken back to the States, he was sent to Dick Donnelly to be schooled. Owner and trainer watched the big gelding, 16.2 hands high, put riderless over a straw-covered hurdle in a long, inclosed chute with seven-foot sides and ends. Suddenly Heatherbloom, deciding he had had lesson enough for the day, leaped a lofty end barrier and trotted to his stall, waiting to be let in.

It was then the astonished watchers realized they had a horse born with the jumping ability which manifests itself as mysteriously in horses as genius in human beings. It has cropped up in such unlikely horseflesh as a pony, a coal wagon nag, and an aged thoroughbred without previous jumping experience.

Heatherbloom began his triumphant tours of the horse shows east and west. As soon as he was through with those harum-scarum entrances of his and preliminary high jinks in the ring, he addressed himself to the jumps. Spectators saw the horse's frank, open countenance take on "an expression at once serene and beatific." He never lost it as he dashed over the course and flew over the seven-foot rails. Often he jumped out of his stride to cover width as well as height. Between the hoofprints of one of his take-offs and his landing was measured a distance of thirty-seven feet. He established a world high-jump record of seven feet, nine inches, then broke it clearing seven feet, ten and one-half inches.

For all his feats in the show ring, Heatherbloom's owner and rider believed he never yet had leaped his limit. At Gedney Farm one day, they decided to see what the big bay really could do in an unofficial trial. Warmed up, he was put at a jump. Over he flashed. Higher went the bars, and Heatherbloom smashed his own world record. Still more bars were hoisted up until the last one was level with the top of the uprights.

Pounding of hoofs ended in the breathless silence of the take-off. The beautiful body soared upward and over through the arc of its trajectory. Without even ticking, Heatherbloom had cleared a towering eight feet, three inches!

Paul Brown

JIM

HE RANG THE FIRE GONG

IN some celestial pasture, where good horses go, Jim must be grazing contentedly. Or, more likely, he munches oats in his stall in a neat, familiar building, imaging the one he knew in life. Suddenly bells beat out a signal. Jim snorts and rushes to his place in front of the gleaming engine. Suspended harness drops on his broad back. He reaches up and with his teeth tugs the rope of the bunk-room gong. Down the pole slide firemen, as Jim neighs impatiently. The driver climbs to his seat. The watchman snaps on Jim's and his teammates' reins and collars, and out they roll.

You say there are no fires in heaven? They're in the other place. Well, there must be make-believe ones then, for the thrilling gallops to smoke-billowing blazes were Jim's idea of heaven on earth.

Jim, a member of Engine Company 17, New York City, was a big fellow—strong enough to pull his share of an engine weighing four tons with firemen aboard, but fast and sure-footed, too. His was the heyday of fire horses: the late 90's and the first two decades of the 1900's. The volunteer firemen,

who ran on foot to fires, hauling their pump-engines, had long since yielded to horses but only after a cholera epidemic decimated their ranks.

Jim, clever and independent, would not wait to be watered when he was thirsty. He undid his strap with his teeth, strolled over to the trough, nuzzled the tap open, and drank, nor did he forget to turn off the water. His pride in a quick start to a fire was no less than his company's. Frequent rehearsals kept getaways well under twenty seconds from the sounding of an alarm and sometimes brought them down to as low as five seconds. Once out the door, Engine 17 really rolled. All his career, Jim lived up to the great tradition of the pioneer engine team which in 1828 made a long, fast run from Yorkville to a raging conflagration in the Bowery.

But as time passed, roughshod though Jim was, his hoofs weakened under the terrific strain of pounding gallops over paved streets. Few fire horses lasted much more than six years, unless they were moved to country stations, with runs over dirt roads. For Jim, like the rest, came the inevitable, sorrowful moment when he and his friends of the company must part. No men ever loved horses more than the firemen of horse-drawn days, but funds were not provided for retirement, and the veteran animals had to be sold at auction.

Records have been destroyed, and the end of Jim's story is unknown. One hopes he found a kind master.

Sometimes fire captains dug up sums they could ill afford to buy an old favorite. A well-to-do New Yorker now and then bid in whole lots of the veterans and sent them into happy retirement on his upstate farm. Perhaps it was Jim's destiny, in common with many of his companions, to be sold to a trades-man and spend the rest of his life pulling a milk wagon or truck. Then Jim, as happened with old fire "plugs," may have staged one of those revivals for which New York streets were often the setting.

Picture him, after he has been sold on the block, plodding along in the shafts of a delivery wagon. It's a dull job, com-pared to the one he knew, but he puts his big shoulders into the collar and pulls steadily. From the avenue yonder sound shrieking whistles and clanging gongs, and Jim's ears prick forward. He sees the fire chief's buggy flash by, then an engine, its team at full gallop, its nickel glistening, red wheels spin-ning, chimney belching smoke. A lurch, and Jim is off to the fire.

He has the bit in his teeth, and there's no stopping him. The driver prudently jumps from the clattering wagon, as it careens around a corner. Hosemen hooking on to a hydrant in front of a burning building look up to recognize an old fire horse, rushing up with his driverless rig to halt beside them, and welcome him with cheers. Jim, for a brief, bright moment, has come back home.

WEX

A POLICE HORSE WENT TO SEA

SURF was booming on the beach at Coney Island, New York, when a cavalcade of policemen in bathing suits, all riding bareback, galloped toward the water, sand spurting from flying hoofs. The long black manes and tails of their horses streamed in the wind. Trim bays, matching beautifully, these geldings were between 15.2 and 16.1 hands high, and any crack cavalry troop would have envied these riders their mounts. This dash into the sea was part of the course of a police horse training school near by.

Foremost was one of the smaller horses, distinguished by a white star in the center of his forehead and black points. Some of the others hesitated to enter the breaking waves; most horses are fine swimmers but dread being overturned in the water since they have difficulty righting themselves. Not so Wex— he plunged in and swam joyously as if the sea were no less his element than the land. The patrolman on his back made a mental note. Such amphibious ability might come in handy some day.

In school, Wex got all his other lessons down pat. He

learned to stand in the middle of a street, with streams of traffic swirling around him—to step out in rhythmic tread and perfect alignment behind a blaring brass band in parades, never shying at fluttering paper—to overtake wild runaways, pressing in close till his master could grasp reins behind the bit—to endure, unflinching, shouts and screams and gunfire in riots—to respond to his master's urging legs and shove back crowds with his broad bay chest. In short, Wex passed his tests with the high honors a horse must earn to become a member of the Mounted Division of the New York Police Force.

Wex's division, the 72nd Precinct, Sheepshead Bay, covered a lot of territory, including waterfront. He and his master were patrolling the beach one day when a small boat, well off-shore, capsized. The rower floundered about, obviously unable to swim even enough to reach his boat and cling to it. There was no life-saving station in the vicinity and no other craft in sight. Down to the sea in long strides galloped the patrol-man.

Wex breasted the surf like one of Neptune's own sea horses. Head just above the surface, he swam steadily through tossing waves. Circling the drowning man, the rider leaned over, grasped him by the collar. Wex headed in and towed like a tugboat until his hoofs struck ground, and the patrolman swung from the saddle to drag the gasping man out on to the sand.

For sixteen years Wex served faithfully in rain and broiling sun, through drifted snow and on icy pavements where he had need of the steel caulks in his shoes to keep his footing. When he was twenty-one, the time came for his retirement. It was 1929, and for some years the auction block and an uncertain and often dismal fate had ceased to be the hard lot of old police horses. The gratitude of citizens and loyalty of the Mounted Division had put a provision in the city's code that transferred retired horses to the custody of the American Society for the Prevention of Cruelty to Animals. The Society disposes of them to some carefully investigated applicant, who promises in writing that the horse shall be used for no purpose for which he is unfitted and shall be given a good home and kind treatment. Horses are regarded only as a loan and must be returned on demand should it be discovered that they are suffering any abuse.

As in the case of other handsome veterans of the Force, there was no lack of applicants for Wex. His new home was a country place on Long Island where he was used for riding. Only one other destiny might perhaps have been happier. Mounted patrolmen, reaching retirement, not infrequently ask for the horses they rode on duty. Wex, one cannot doubt, would have loved to spend the rest of his life with one of his old masters of the Force.

BLACK GOLD

UNDER A STAR OF ILL OMEN

ACROSS the Oklahoma sky, the night the black colt was foaled, a shooting star blazed a fiery trail. The Osage Indian, H. M. Hoots, who owned the new-born creature, stared upward and shook his head in super-stitious dread. To be born under such a comet was a sign of bad luck, he muttered. And so it proved. This colt, by Black Toney out of Useeit, would meet disaster and bring it upon men who had to do with him, like the Seian horse of the Romans.

The Osage himself was the first victim. He did not live to see the colt, named Black Gold after the rich oil bubbling from the earth of his native State, win races for him like his dam. A few days after the foal's birth, Hoots, never sick before in his life, died suddenly.

Then for a while the star hid its baleful light. Black Gold, small but sturdy, began to show such speed as a two-year-old that he was entered in the Louisiana Derby. Drenched by a cold rain on the New Orleans Fair Ground track, heavy with mud, the fleet little black galloped into the lead, held it all the way and won at 50 to 1.

Paul Brown

His odds were down to 10 to 1 when he was started in the Kentucky Derby in 1924 and faced the fastest three-year-olds in the land. Throngs roared, as he flashed out in front at the stretch and won, going away. Yet the jinx caught many who had backed him heavily, for hard-hit bookmakers welched on their bets.

A weakness had developed in Black Gold's near foreleg. After a race's ordeal, he stood trembling and suffering in his stall. He limped after every time trial but, treated and bandaged, he was always ready for the next event. Coming from twenty lengths behind in the Chicago Derby, he ticked off the field one by one to sweep through to victory in the last hundred yards. That year he ran thirteen races, and the gallant little stallion won nine of them on a game leg and a courageous heart.

Now he was retired to stud, but his fateful star shone again. Black Gold was sterile. Ill fortune was also the lot of the jockey who had ridden him to victory on Churchill Downs; unable to keep his weight down, he could find no better job than exercise boy. Hard luck dogged the black's trainers as well; their stables produced no more winners. Just as the tide began to turn for one trainer, he died.

But Black Gold's owners were not ready to discard a Derby winner as a hoodoo horse. There were fat purses to be won, and rest must have helped his game leg, they reasoned. So in 1928 he came to the post again on the scene of his first triumph, the Louisiana Derby, and the stands, remembering, gave him a rousing greeting.

Up clicked the barrier, hoofs drummed, and Black Gold was off and away with his old-time dash. At the half-mile post, he swung wide out of the ruck and went after the pace-maker. But coming into the home stretch, his steady stride faltered. He staggered, lurched but still struggled on. Then he crashed to the turf. His game limb had snapped, and even a valiant horse cannot run far on a broken leg. A veterinarian's hypodermic needle gave him a merciful death.

A granite monument marks his grave in the infield of the Fair Grounds track. Upon its shaft each year after the Derby is run, the winning jockey places his wreath in heart-warming tribute to Black Gold.

MAN O' WAR

BIG RED

HE raced in the airplane age and
lived through the day when jet planes outsped sound. Only a
moderate rate for an automobile was the record he made when
he covered a quarter at around forty-three miles per hour. Yet
that was faster than any horse ever had been known to run,
and men who saw his mighty stride and glorious action as he
galloped around a track, always will acclaim him king of speed.

Man O' War was the timely name given him when he was
foaled in the stable of Major August Belmont in 1917, with
cannon thundering across the Atlantic. Sired by a fleet race-
horse, Fair Play, out of Mahubah, his pedigree traced back
two and a half centuries through twenty-two generations. But
his long-legged, big-boned frame, 16½ hands, lent him an awk-
ward look, and at the sale where Samuel D. Riddle bid him
in for $5000, other yearlings fetched almost thrice that price.

Because of his size and ruddy, chestnut coat, stable-boys on
the Riddle farm called him Big Red. To Trainer Louis Feustel
and Foreman George Conway he was just another colt of no

Paul Brown

particular promise. Big Red developed power—figuratively and actually "he ate like a horse"—and he liked to run, though he was a slow-starter. Crafty training eliminated that fault. Man O' War, otherwise an equine gentleman, got tough at the barrier, jostling and rearing to go and bound not to be left at the post.

He won small races and went on to capture big ones with those gigantic strides of his—two feet longer than the average thoroughbred's and once measured at twenty-eight feet. During his first year on the track, he lost a race for the first and last time in his life when he got off to a bad start and was beaten by a horse, appropriately named in the light of subsequent events, Upset.

World records for various distances fell beneath Man O' War's flying hoofs. The huge crowds he drew loved him and cheered the stirring spectacle of that chestnut streak flashing over a course. Jockeys in Sam Riddle's black and gold strained to hold him in to keep him from winning by so many lengths it would make the field look ridiculous. He earned nearly $240,-000 in purses, becoming the greatest money-winner in American racing up to that time. Odds on Big Red plummeted until they were 1 to 100 against him at the Belmont Stakes. Man O' War breezed in ahead by twenty lengths. Only once was his pre-eminence seriously challenged. At Aqueduct, John P. Grier ran nose-and-nose with him, while world's records toppled at every furlong pole, and was leading by a neck when they came into the stretch. Then the chestnut hide felt the rare

flick of a jockey's whip, and Big Red catapulted to the fore
to cross the finish line a length and a half ahead.

There were no more worlds to conquer. Retired in his prime
to stud, the champion was bred to the choicest mares at a fee
of $5000. He sired 383 foals, among them not a few who have
carried on his fame from generation to generation. Cakes with
carrot candles signalized his birthdays at his home near Lex-
ington, Kentucky, of which he was made an honorary citizen.
Selected sculptors and painters were permitted to portray him.
For years he received the pilgrimage of several thousand visi-
tors a month. Until his death in 1947 at thirty—equivalent to
a human age of ninety—he accepted homage in calm dignity
when his faithful Negro groom, Will Harbutt, presented him
to admirers: "Ladies and gentlemen, here is 'the mostest hoss
in the world.' Here is Man O' War *hisself!*"

GAY BOY

DEATH FROM THE AIR

A MAN may deliberately choose a dangerous career or an adventure where he risks his neck for fame, money, or the thrill of it. A horse's destiny is determined for him by his breeding, by the qualities he develops, by various quirks of fortune. It was Gay Boy's lot to become a polo pony.

His future could not be predicted at the outset. Although the sire of the bay colt, foaled in Texas, was blooded, his dam was an ordinary range mare. Yet the qualities he began to display increased the certainty that he would play the ancient game from out of Asia, his trim hoofs beating the tattoo of headlong gallops over the greensward, his ears pricked to catch the click of mallet on ball. Gay Boy was fast and alert, so quick to wheel and follow the bounding white sphere that he reminded you of a hawk swooping on its prey. And his mother's rugged strength in him gave promise of staying powers.

The half-bred bay gelding joined the élite when he was bought for the stables of W. Averell Harriman, wealthy owner of two large polo pony studs. That keen sportsman, who often generously mounted players on the American team for matches

with the British, lent Gay Boy to Malcom Stevenson for the Internationals of 1924.

Willing, swift to sense commands by leg or rein almost before he felt their pressure—that was Gay Boy. And he was utterly fearless. In lightning races after the ball, he never shrank from imminent collisions, and in ride-offs he gave and took more than his quota of the twenty to fifty body-checks a polo pony meets in a game. Not he but an Argentine mare was being played when an accident put Stevenson out of action. Making a rapid turn, the mare crossed her forelegs, and her rider was thrown, suffering a brain concussion.

Gay Boy was lent R. E. Strawbridge, Jr., for the 1927 International Matches. In one game the pony played through two entire periods and through three in another—a rare exhibition of stamina in which the bay gave his all till the last moment.

For more than a decade polo players called Gay Boy "tops." He faced and survived all the game's hazards. It was not in the stars for him to be killed in a match like another Harriman pony, Applesauce, which is buried with honor beneath the Sands Point goal posts. Gay Boy was doomed to a strange end.

One day in 1928 he stood in his stable quietly munching hay. In the sky sounded the thunder of something swifter— and less dependable—than he. Two Army aviators were testing a plane. Suddenly its wings buckled. The flyers bailed out, to descend safely by parachute, but the plane plummeted through the stable's roof, crushing Gay Boy and another polo pony.

MIDNIGHT

PRIDE OF RODEOS

THEY called him Midnight, since he was black as the twelfth hour, with no moon and not a single star twinkling. Foaled on an Alberta ranch, he was raised as a regular cow pony, but riding herd plainly did not appeal to Midnight. The black colt was roped, snubbed to a fence-post for a saddle to be cinched on, and a rider climbed aboard. When ropes were loosed, the fireworks started, as Midnight exploded into violent action. The cowpuncher shot into the air and lit with a thud in the dust of the corral.

Well, the young ones from off the range all pitched at first. Cattlemen said it was in their blood—inherited from their forebears of the wild herds. Those mustangs, descended from Spanish steeds, had learned how when a mountain lion sprang from a tree-branch ambush on to their backs. Then it was pitch him off in a hurry before savage jaws broke their necks or a clawing hind foot disemboweled them.

Most bucking horses gave up soon and behaved. Not Midnight—he piled every cowhand that forked him. In the old days, such broncos were shot and left to the buzzards or used for wolf bait, but not in the 1920's, with rodeos rating as one of the most profitable branches of show business. Midnight showed signs of a talent that might make him a more valuable property than whole herds of ordinary cow ponies.

When he was three, Midnight was started on his tours of the Wild West show and rodeo circuits. Twist the ballad slightly and you had Midnight's theme song: *Give a Man a Horse He Can't Ride*. The Canadian colt was that horse. With some ambitious bronco-buster's legs wrapped around him, he flashed out of the chute and lived up to his billing as a black keg of dynamite. Pitching, corkscrewing, sunfishing, swapping ends, Midnight staged all the tricks of his trade. "He had a belly full of bed-springs," as the saying went. Pull leather or not, nobody stayed long on that hurricane deck. With a rueful rider staring up at him from the ground, Midnight gleefully kicked his heels until he was picked up for the next competitor unlucky enough to draw him. When he was stabled after his day's work, the "devil horse" turned gentle as a lamb. Anybody on the place could walk up to him in the pasture, halter him and ride him down to the corral for water.

For fourteen years, Midnight performed throughout the United States, Canada, and in England, and tossed the best riders, while his owners cashed in handsomely. At last in 1933, when he was seventeen, he was ridden twice at Fort Worth, Texas.

All great actors past their prime should be retired. Midnight, awarded a well-earned rest—roaming the range in sum-

Paul Brown

mer, a warm stall in winter—died at the age of twenty and was buried at Platteville, Colorado, beneath a headstone. Inscribed upon it is this "Verse by a Cowboy."

Under this sod lies a great bucking hoss.
There never lived a cowboy he couldn't toss.
His name was Midnight,
His coat black as coal.
If there is a hoss heaven,
Please God rest his soul.

ELKRIDGE

HE WON BY A HEAD

HE ran with his head, as well as with heart and sinews, in the most dangerous, exhausting and thrilling of all horse races: the steeplechase. Elkridge came to know the great American courses—Belmont, Pimlico, Saratoga, and the rest—as a general does a battleground of his choosing, and he employed tactics and strategy to win. His jockeys learned to leave him in command.

When Elkridge was foaled in Maryland in 1938 and named for a noted hunt club of the State, a career lay clear before him. Let the blue grass of Kentucky nourish the fleet flat racers. The Maryland thoroughbred will be, like Nimrod, the son of Cush in the Scriptures, a mighty hunter before the Lord, a point-to-pointer, or a steeplechaser. So it has been from the days of Lord Baltimore and his hard-riding Cavaliers.

Trained as a 'chaser, the bay gelding developed quickly. Not large—he stood only a little over 15.3—his were the strength and stamina his calling requires. Like other racers, he was given a stable companion, a brindled Great Dane named Buck, at once his mascot and bodyguard. Buck would beat a tolerant retreat before a spitting kitten but had to be chained when the veterinary came, or he would have flown at his throat. The big dog knew that treatments sometimes hurt the horse that was his friend.

As a three-year-old, Elkridge claimed his birthright and began to carry the colors of his owner, Kent Miller, to victory, winning so often he became the top steeplechaser of 1942. That first year his jockeys discovered that Elkridge ran races his own way and they were only along for the ride. Sometimes he made the pace throughout, but usually he preferred to come from behind in the last half-mile. Jockeys up on the other entries looked back apprehensively over their shoulders to see him come galloping up abreast. His thundering rush threw their leg-weary mounts out of stride, forcing them to take off badly or overjump. Triumphantly Elkridge passed them, flew the last fences and sped down the stretch to the finish.

Rough handling or anything he regarded as discourtesy was likely to make Elkridge temperamental. In one race, an assistant starter so annoyed him that he sulked all the way around the course. Nothing his jockey could do would persuade him really to run. He finished in the ruck, and his unfortunate rider was put down by the judges for ten days for not trying.

But such moods were rare. Out of ninety-five starts in eight years of steeplechasing, Elkridge won or placed fifty times. At the age of ten, carrying top weights, he established a track record at Saratoga and equaled it in his next start. Since steeplechase stakes are far lower than for flat races, Elkridge's winnings of more than $169,000 were remarkable.

Paul Brown

Greater than victories or earnings was another achievement by Elkridge. Although he lost his rider four times, when he hit fences or swerved to avoid a competitor that had crashed, never once in his many races did the sure-footed bay fall.

CITATION

TRIUMPH AND A THREE-YEAR-OLD

HIS air was regal, yet without a trace of arrogance, as he surveyed the crowds lining rails and cramming stands, come to watch him race. You could describe his direct gaze and the proud way he held his head by that fine phrase which is the title of a great horse story, "The Look of Eagles." When Citation flashed around a track and forged in front of the field, effortless power in his long stride, he often stared upward over the tree tops at the sky, as if he were about to take flight.

Foaled in 1945, by Bull Lea out of the English mare, Hydroplane II, blood was the first token of triumph for the big colt, his coat gleaming with the sheen of rich mahogany and three of his feet tipped with white. Good fortune bestowed two other factors: a fine trainer, Jimmy Jones, and expert jockeys. As a two-year-old, Citation commenced to gather laurels wholesale for the Calumet Farm stables of his owner, Warren Wright, and swept onward into his great third year.

Race after race fell to his flying hoofs, though twice he was nosed out and, crestfallen, had to be content with second

place. Rarely did he feel the flick of a whip. A cluck by his
jockey was enough to tap that mighty reservoir of power and
shoot him into the lead with a momentum that carried him, far
ahead, over the finish. With Eddie Arcaro up, Citation became
the eighth horse in history to capture the triple crown of the
Kentucky Derby, the Preakness, and the Belmont Stakes. In
twenty-seven starts, he chalked up twenty-five victories. By
October, 1948, his winnings had mounted to $830,250, and he
was moving up toward Stymie's world-record earnings of
$911,335.

Citation bore himself like the king of the turf he was, yet
even monarchs relax at home. Along with other great race
horses, his favorite stable companion was a cat, and a cat pro-
verbially can look at a king. Citation's feline friend did more
than look. These two frequently played together. The cat would
climb up and begin to steal along a bar at the rear of the stall.
Swiftly the bay whirled and tried to push his mascot off her
perch with his muzzle before she could run across. Again and
again the pair would play through their game.

They were calling Citation as great as Man O' War and
greater when he was entered for the Pimlico Special at the end
of the 1948 season. There occurred his most impressive triumph
of all. Citation was the only entry. Not a horse in the nation
was considered to have a chance against him.

It was like a tournament of the days when knighthood was
in flower. Citation entered the lists as the champion. An an-
nouncer, in the character of a herald, proclaimed his puissance

Paul Brown

and read the roll of his victories, while applause greeted the handsome bay's stately parade. One could almost imagine him casting a shoe in defiance, as knights of old flung down a gauntlet. And not one challenger came forth.

In gleaming silks, Eddie Arcaro rode him to the barrier, alone except for his stablemate pony. Spectators grinned as they saw Citation stare about him wonderingly. None could doubt what thoughts were running through that tossing head. Where was the opposition? Were no other horses going to race him? Was this to be just a gallop for exercise or against time? No matter—it was fun to run.

They didn't bother with a gate but just flagged Citation off in the start. Arcaro took his mount past the stands in slow motion, as if to display his beauty and symmetry in action. Taut reins on the overcheck bit relaxed a little at the stretch (jockeys seldom let the racer go all-out) and to the cheers of the crowd Citation thundered over the line, with the rest of the field—very literally—nowhere. In the winner's paddock he flung out his heels with elation and just missed an admiring policeman.

Even in his third year, Citation was a horse of destiny.

48
44

N